D1055654

An Irish Nature Year

Jane Powers

WILLIAM
COLLINS

William Collins
An imprint of HarperCollins*Publishers*
1 London Bridge Street
London SE1 9GF

WilliamCollinsBooks.com

HarperCollins*Publishers*
1st Floor, Watermarque Building, Ringsend Road
Dublin 4, Ireland

First published in Great Britain by William Collins in 2020

2021 2023 2022
4 6 8 10 9 7 5 3

ISBN 978-0-00-839214-7

Typeset in Berling by Jacqui Caulton
Printed and bound in Great Britain by CPI Group (UK) Ltd, Croydon

MIX
Paper from
responsible sources
FSC™ C007454
FSC
www.fsc.org

In memory of Hugh Wahl Powers,
a friend to Irish nature

Contents

Introduction

Nature is all around us. We don't have to be walking in the countryside or wandering along a beach. It is there, even in the built-up corners of cities. It is in the ivy-leaved toadflax tumbling from a wall crevice, in the chatter of house sparrows sheltering in a neglected hedge, in the clouds of ants appearing mysteriously on a still, summer afternoon. Nature is a constant friend, but so omnipresent that we often forget to admire it and be thankful for its existence.

In these daily notes, I have attempted to give a quick reminder of what is happening in the natural world. Some of the observations relate to creatures and plants that are on our doorsteps, some that are farther afield, and some that even share our living quarters (say 'hello' to the long-bodied cellar spider). All the flora and fauna mentioned here can be seen from dry land. You don't need any special equipment to view it, but if you can get your hands on a magnifying glass and a pair of binoculars, you will see closer, deeper, farther.

Ireland, although it is a relatively small island, has an endlessly interesting flora and fauna. Our climate, with its abundant moisture and lack of extreme temperatures, favours plant growth in every month of the year, so there is always something noteworthy going on in nature. Migrant birds from colder regions visit in winter, confident that our shorelines will give them sustenance through the chilly months. Our western coast abuts the Atlantic Ocean where nature is at its wildest and most magnificent. Whales can be seen from the headlands, as can basking sharks, the gentle giants of the fish world. Some of our plants and animals are bafflingly absent from Britain, our nearest neighbour. Yet, they occur in Ireland, as well as parts of the Mediterranean and in the northwest of Spain and Portugal. Among these are the Kerry slug, the Kerry lily and Saint Patrick's cabbage. Collectively these species are known as the Lusitanian biota (after the area of the Iberian peninsula where some are concentrated, a region that was once the Roman province of Lusitania). The reason for this anomaly is unclear. But its presence adds to the singular magic of our land.

Much of my writing life has been devoted to gardens and gardening, but I have always had a *grá* for nature. I can't help but admire the elastic slugs that eat my lettuces; the satisfyingly baroque form of the shieldbugs on the raspberries; and the portly bullfinches that rip petals from the apple trees. And as for wildflowers, I love their wayward characters. Unlike garden plants, which we subjugate to serve us, wild plants have minds of their own. They do no-one's bidding and they go exactly where they want – which is always the best place for their particular needs and attributes. If we want to see them and understand them, we must go and visit them on their own terms. For this reason, I will happily go on my knees in a damp bog to commune with the flowers of an orchid or saxifrage.

Wild plants mean different things to different people. Our ancestors variously worshipped them, feared them, told stories about them. They collected them to eat, to flavour food and drink, to use as dyes, as tools, as textiles. They made remedies for themselves and their animals. They named their towns and villages after them. Holly (*cuileann* in Irish) gives us Glencullen in Dublin and Moycullen in Galway, while birch (*beith*) gives us Glenbeigh in Kerry and Ballybay in Monaghan. Other placenames commemorate bramble, heather and oak, to mention just three species. Plants themselves have many vernacular names, each specific to an area. Foxglove has at least two dozen names in English (including fairy thimbles and dead man's fingers), and around the same number in Irish, among them, the simply descriptive *lus mór* – 'great herb', as in a very large plant.

We have fewer animal species in Ireland than many other regions, but we have some that are special. Our Irish hare is a subspecies of the white Arctic hare; our coal tits are also unique, with warmly toned cheek patches.

In the daily offerings in this book, I have tried to capture some of the infinite interestingness of nature in Ireland. There is an entire world in a layer of damp leaves, in the corrugated bark of an oak tree and in the small rock pool that appears at low tide. Nature finds innumerable niches in which to set up its different species, in communities that mesh perfectly together. Sometimes we forget that we humans are part of the picture. But we are, and our actions have huge effects – beneficial or otherwise – on the animals and plants that we share this planet with. We are the world's most invasive species, a label that isn't my or your fault, but we can, nonetheless, each do our bit to soften our impact. In the back of the book, you'll find websites and other resources: organisations to join and advice to follow. The more we learn the lighter our step.

A note on safety and consideration: In this book the old remedies that I mention are given only as a matter of historical interest, and are definitely not recommended. If you are foraging for berries or other foods, don't eat anything unless you know it is safe. Always leave plenty for birds and other animals, and never forage in nature reserves. Don't pick wildflowers: insects and other creatures depend on them for food and shelter. Take photos if you want to identify species at home. Collect lichens, mosses, nuts, cones and seashells *only* if they have been dislodged already. Be moderate in your collecting and gentle with your footsteps.

A note on the text: Some of the material in this book appeared in my daily column in *The Times Ireland*.

January

1st On New Year's Day, there are plenty of flowers in bloom, and the simple lawn daisy is the most frequently seen. The name is derived from 'day's-eye', because the flowers open with the morning light and close at dusk. This protects the flower from the elements during the hours of darkness, when there are no pollinators about. An old custom was for children to pick as many daisies as they could, and to go from door to door demanding a 'penny for the daisy'. In recent years, the Botanical Society of Britain and Ireland has run a new year plant hunt, open to everyone. Participants count – but don't collect – as many wild plants in flower as possible during a period of up to three hours and upload the results to the society's website (bsbi.org). In mild years, hundreds of species may be in flower, some early, some late. Other plants commonly in bloom now include groundsel, dandelion, annual meadow grass, shepherd's purse, chickweed and purple dead-nettle.

2nd Winter trees lack leaves, but some are still easy to identify. Ash trees are hung with messy bunches of 'keys' and have smooth grey twigs with black buds. Beech branches are also smooth and grey, but the twigs are a warm brown and are punctuated with alternate, tightly rolled buds, like tiny cigars. Horse chestnut buds are plump, deep red and sticky. Cast your eye down the stem and look for the marks left behind when last year's leaves fell: they are shaped like horseshoes, and even have 'nail holes' around the edges. Hazel and alder are bearing catkins. Birch may be farther behind with its own catkins, but its milky bark and dark, flexible-twigged branches are obvious. The slim and whippy red-orange twigs of willow are especially cheering when lit by the low winter light. Oak trees have deeply corrugated bark and a generous, spreading shape. Look around their bases for the corky little berets that once covered their acorns.

3rd As the weather gets colder, and as food supplies dwindle in their usual territories, lesser redpolls come visiting Irish gardens. These little birds breed in upland and bog-edge forestry, often in conifers. They move to lower and more productive ground as winter progresses, sometimes arriving in gregarious parties with other small birds, including tits, siskins and goldcrests. They are the smallest members of the finch family, weighing in at between eleven and sixteen grams, the same as two or three heaped teaspoons of sugar. They are sweet little things, streaked delicately with brown and beige. Mature birds have a wee black *smig*, and – true to their name – crimson blotches on their foreheads which become more pronounced as the season progresses and the feathers wear away. Some sport fine rosy chests. Nyjer seed is a sure way to entice them into a garden. They are delightfully acrobatic, hanging off birch and alder catkins, and even from the seedheads of ornamental grasses.

4th Clearing the garden in this season can reveal various insects and other creepy-crawlies that have tucked themselves away for winter. Parties of aphids camp on evergreen plants, such as spurges and wallflowers, and provide much-needed fuel for little birds, including tits and wrens. Some insects cluster under the bark of trees, especially on the south-facing side where they are warmed by the sun. Others shelter under rocks or in the stalks of dead plants. Tap a dried, hollow stem and woodlice and earwigs may fall out. Both overwinter as adults: woodlice can live two to four years, while earwigs don't survive much longer than a year. Ladybirds, their legs drawn up tightly inside their red wing cases, nestle in dormancy in dead leaves, in crevices on dry stems, and in sheds and vacant birdhouses. Snails hibernate in groups, glued to the inside of upturned pots and other dry places.

5th We are entering the breeding season for red squirrels. Invasive grey squirrels sometimes have rusty-toned backs, but they are twice the size and lack ear tufts. Reds are tremendously wary, staying up in trees (on the less visible side of trunks and branches) rather than running along the ground in full sight, as greys do. Red squirrels arrived in Ireland first during the Iron Age, when they may have been introduced for their skins. They became extinct or nearly extinct more than once, and those we see today are the descendants of several introductions during the nineteenth century. Red and grey squirrels cannot co-exist, as the latter compete for food: they raid the caches of the former, and they are also able to digest acorns earlier in the season, when they still contain a large amount of tannins. Grey squirrels carry squirrelpox virus, a disease which can cause them no harm, but which is fatal for reds. A recent resurgence of pine martens is probably helping to reduce numbers of greys, which allows the red squirrel population to recover.

6th If you are feeding a large population of little birds such as finches and tits, chances are that you are also feeding at least one sparrowhawk. Despite the name, the principal food of this common bird of prey is not sparrows. It is more likely to be blue tits, or – if you have a nyjer seed dispenser – goldfinches. Sparrowhawks attack in the blink of an eye. Often all we see is a split-second shadow-bird, followed by a suddenly deserted feeding station, with perhaps a forlornly drifting feather. The sparrowhawk avoids being spotted on its way to a strike by flying low to the ground.

It can accelerate to fifty kilometres an hour, swerving through small spaces by pulling its wings close to its rocket-like body. The female is considerably larger than the opposite sex, and can easily take down a wood pigeon. In times of scarcity, she may even dispatch a male sparrowhawk.

7th Occasionally, wasps are out and about on warmer winter days. These are most likely to be young queens who mated in autumn and who normally hibernate in crevices in walls and trees, or in attics. Milder temperatures, however, may rouse them. This can be fatal, as there is little food available for them. Hundreds of queens leave each colony, but only a handful survive to set up their own nests in spring. Some are killed by predators such as spiders, while others starve. A folk story says that when Jesus, Mary and Joseph were fleeing to Egypt, a wasp who had seen them told Herod's soldiers that they had passed by on that day. A cricket, however, who was more sympathetic to the family's plight and wanted to confuse the pursuers, said it had been the previous day. For this reason, there is a saying that wasps should be killed, but crickets spared. In reality, wasps are the allies of humans, as they feed on aphids and other crop-eating insects.

8th Barnacle geese from Greenland are with us now, particularly along the northwest coast. They are medium-sized, monochromatic birds, with black breast, necks, bills and legs, white bellies and heads, and barred upper parts. Their colouring is effective camouflage in an arctic environment of dark rocks and snow. Here they are conspicuous, gathering on green fields and salt marshes in their hundreds. In the past, before it was known that they were migrants, people thought they hatched from barnacles, an example of 'nature acting against her own laws', according to Gerald of Wales in his twelfth-century

History and Topography of Ireland. 'They take their food and nourishment from the juice of wood and water during their mysterious and remarkable generation. I myself have seen many times and with my own eyes more than a thousand of these small bird-like creatures hanging from a single log upon the seashore. They were in their shells and already formed.' In fact, he was seeing what is now known as the goose barnacle: a stalked barnacle that colonises driftwood and other floating debris. Gerald went on to note that the clergy in Ireland could eat barnacle geese 'without sin during a fasting time' as they were not 'born of flesh'.

9th Our most dramatic evergreen is the yew, and specifically the Irish yew, the sombre tree that watches darkly over churchyards, and offers shelter to roosting birds. All Irish yews are descendants of a pair found around 1760 on the side of Cuilcagh Mountain in County Fermanagh. The finder, George Willis, gave one to his landlord, Lord Enniskillen, at nearby Florence Court. The nonconformist seedlings had an upright, columnar ('fastigiate') shape, completely different from the spreading branches of the normal species, *Taxus baccata*. The original Florence Court yew, which still exists, is female, but the seeds almost invariably produce non-fastigiate trees. The only way to reliably make a new Irish yew is to take cuttings from one. This means that the Fermanagh tree is the mother of millions of Irish yews. Almost all those in existence throughout the world were propagated from her or her clones. The fact that there were no mature Irish yews before the end of the eighteenth century gives great pleasure to those who like to pick holes in the authenticity of period films and television series – which regularly feature them in gardens and graveyards.

10th Waterfowl numbers are at their peak this month. Among the ducks that you might see in the calm, shallow water of estuaries and flooded fields is the shoveler. It is well named, with a great, utilitarian, black bill that gives the bird a self-conscious look. Males have bold and contrasting plumage with a dark-green head, chestnut-brown sides, and black and white flashes on front and rear. The colours are roughly similar to those of the shelduck, but the shoveler has a greater expanse of chestnut, and is much smaller and squatter. Close up, that great Wellington boot of a bill is unmistakable. Its purpose is to filter mouthfuls of water. Fine filaments inside the bill catch plankton, crustaceans and other aquatic foods when the water is ejected. Shovelers sometimes feed with their bottoms in the air, when you can see their long wing feathers crossed over their plasticky orange-red feet. Most of our wintering birds are visitors from France, northern Europe, the Baltic and western Russia, while a few come from Iceland. Shovelers breed here in small numbers – mainly around Lough Neagh, the Shannon basin and on coastal estuaries.

11th Alders have dropped all their leaves, but their branches are not bare. Bunches of juvenile male catkins dangle from the ends of the twigs like tiny knitted sausages. They will open in early spring and release their pollen. Last year's female catkins, which resemble minute pine cones, are still on the trees. Their oil-rich nutlets are carefully winkled out by finches and goldcrests. Alder often grows alongside rivers, where the roots help to stabilise the banks. The seeds are adapted to float on water: each one has little pockets of air that keep it buoyant for up to a year. It may germinate during that time, and when it hits land it quickly establishes as a sapling. Alder wood also has water-resistant properties and if kept wet, will withstand rot. Some of the piles that support buildings and bridges in Venice are made from alder. The cones of *Alnus glutinosa* are sometimes added to ornamental fish tanks. They lower the pH of the water by releasing tannins and thus help prevent fungal and bacterial infection of fish eggs.

12th Sometimes, just before dusk, you may pass a dense evergreen tree or shrub that seems to shimmer and chatter. This is the roosting place of a colony of talkative house sparrows. Their brownish plumage makes them nearly invisible in the shadowy depths. Some birds, such as starlings, travel twenty to thirty kilometres each evening to join their roosts. Not house sparrows, however, who usually spend their entire lives within a few kilometres from where they were hatched. Although they won't be nesting for another couple of months, males are beginning to show their breeding colours, as the grey tips of their autumn-acquired plumage wear away to reveal darker and more contrasting tones. Their sex organs, which shrank to next to nothing over winter are in the process of swelling to working dimensions: about the size of a chickpea. When fully developed, a house sparrow's testes weigh in at over two per cent of his body mass. Proportionately, this is twice the size of a chicken's testes, and over seven times those of a turkey.

13th January is not a month we normally associate with the mushroom tribe. Yet this is the season when the jelly ear fungus is looking its best. The fleshy, liver-coloured growths appear on dead and dying wood, most often on elder, and occasionally on other trees, including sycamore and beech. The 'ears' always grow facing downwards, so you need to view them from underneath to observe the oval shape and fleshy folds that confer on them their name. Some can look realistically and creepily ear-like – which always pleases younger nature lovers. They are most visible in winter, as they may be dehydrated at other times. When the sun shines through them, they become a warm, caramel colour, which is nicely complemented by their velvety upper surface. The fungus is also known as wood ear, and formerly as Jew's ear, which is reflected in the Latin specific epithet: *Auricularia auricula-judae*. Another older name is Judas's ear. This is because Judas Iscariot was said to have hanged himself on an elder tree.

14th Ducks, waders, gulls and other water birds spend a great deal of time with their feet in very cold water. Yet, although they are warm-blooded creatures, they appear to feel no ill effects. Instead of bouncing up and down, or avoiding icy water altogether, they are entirely comfortable. Nature has arranged that their legs and feet are maintained at a much cooler temperature than the body core. Accordingly, there is very little heat loss, even in freezing conditions. A mechanism known as 'countercurrent circulation' keeps the blood in the feet cool and that in the body warm. This is a natural heat exchange system between closely placed blood vessels. The arteries, which carry warm blood from the core, pass alongside veins carrying cold blood from the feet. Arterial blood is cooled by the adjacent cold veins, and the venous blood is heated up by the warm arteries. By the time the arterial blood flows into the feet, it has transferred almost all its warmth to the venous blood that is travelling upwards. Thus, the body remains warm and the feet cold. Occasional surges of warm blood into the feet keep them from freezing.

15th There is less greenery around now, which makes it a good time to get a clear view of the structure of bramble plants, the givers of wild blackberries. If you could see a time-lapse film taken over a year or two, a shoot would look animate, snaking across the ground and rearing up to climb trees or loop over a wall or hedgerow. Such a stem can progress at 7.5 centimetres per day. The fierce thorns deter animals while also helping the plant to grasp surfaces. When a shoot runs out of steam after several metres, it drops to the ground and presses itself firmly against the soil. Its tip splays out and sends out a set of pale roots. When the roots have gained a foothold, a new shoot springs up and wanders off on its own journey. The larvae of many moths and a few butterflies feed on bramble leaves. At present, holly blue butterfly pupae and emperor moth caterpillars are overwintering on the plants.

16th Feral pigeons are reviled by many and dubbed with unkind nicknames such as 'flying rats' or 'rats with wings'. These birds that inhabit our urban areas are mostly the descendants of racing pigeons that have lost their way or been abandoned. They are a population of dispossessed, redundant athletes, wandering about finding scraps of food wherever they can. This is especially poignant because pigeons were once valiant couriers. During the Second World War, Operation Columba saw sixteen thousand British homing pigeons – all donated by ordinary pigeon fanciers – parachuted in canisters into occupied Europe. A note asked the finders to attach details regarding the state of nearby Nazi troops and to send the pigeon on its way. Over a thousand of these 'spy pigeons' arrived back home. The ancestor of feral pigeons is the European rock dove (*Columba livia*), a few of which still inhabit remote, rocky cliffs along the west of Ireland. Their descendants, accordingly, are comfortable among the hard ledges and roofs of city architecture. Adults make long-lasting pair bonds and may raise several broods per year of one or two chicks, which are called squabs. Both partners share the chore of incubating the eggs and feeding the young on 'pigeon milk', a high-fat, high-protein substance manufactured in the bird's crop.

17th

God in His wisdom made the fly
And then forgot to tell us why.

When Ogden Nash wrote that pithy little poem in 1942, he didn't understand the immense importance of flies and the epic work that they do. Perhaps he didn't know this:

Without them we'd be knee-deep in corpses and faeces
And surely the earth would be falling to pieces.

Flies and their larvae – maggots – are responsible for marvellous feats of waste processing. They are among the many invertebrates that industriously recycle dead or discarded matter into soil nutrients. The role of flies in this world is crucial: without them, our planet would cease functioning. Flies are food for all manner of predators: other invertebrates and birds, fish, reptiles, amphibians and mammals. They are important pollinators: some plants, including chocolate and rare orchids, are pollinated only by members of this under-appreciated order. Hoverflies, with their pretty striped or furry suits, are probably the best-loved of all *Diptera* (from the Greek for two-winged). There are 160,000 known fly species in the world (and thousands unknown). They include everything from tiny midges to great, gangly craneflies.

18th
Despite its name, the grey wagtail is more yellow than grey. While the wings and back are slate-grey, it is the lemon-toned rump and undercarriage that calls attention to the bird, especially when set aglow by the low January sun. This elegant relative of the pied wagtail favours fast-flowing water and wild places, and is rarely seen in gardens. Colder weather, however, drives it to more sheltered areas, so those of us with tiny ponds can sometimes be surprised by its

presence in winter. These garden visitors may be Irish birds or migrants from northern Europe. The grey wagtail is lovely to watch, bouncing in one place as if on springs, while its long tail dips up and down exaggeratedly. In Ireland, it is often known as the yellow wagtail. This is confusing, as the true yellow wagtail is another bird, a rarely seen passage migrant that winters in southern Spain and sub-Saharan Africa.

19th Sometimes, when you are on a beach, you spot a seal out in the sea – just a chimney-cowl of a head, dark against the water. If it is close enough, the black, liquid eyes are visible. Seals are inquisitive and often swim parallel to walkers, especially if there are dogs in tow. We have two native seals: the grey seal and the harbour or common seal. The 'common' is misleading: its population is 4,500 to 5,500 individuals while that of the grey seal is 7,000 to 9,000. Harbour seals are smaller animals, but the two species can be difficult to differentiate when in the water. Harbour seals have a v-shaped nostril configuration and more dog-like heads with a rounded forehead and a dip down to the nose. Grey seals have a smoothly sloped, egg-shaped head, with the look of a more dignified, Roman nose. There is much Irish mythology about seals. Some stories say that they are the souls of dead fishermen, while others say that they are people who were unable to get onto Noah's Ark.

20th Hooded crows are often at the seashore, especially in winter, when there are fewer insects about for them to feed on. When the tide is out, they hunt among seaweedy rocks in the intertidal area – a rich hunting ground revealed when the water retreats. There, they find shellfish such as periwinkles, mussels and cockles. Hoodies or grey crows (*feannóg* and *caróg liath* in Irish) are known for dropping the shells onto hard surfaces to shatter them so they can get at the insides. Researchers studying the activities of thirty-four hooded crows in Cork Harbour discovered that the average height from which adults dropped mussels was 4.8 metres. From around this height, the shells broke and the flesh was easily retrieved. Any higher and more energy would be expended, the contents would spread farther and the bird would spend longer retrieving it, possibly risking plundering from other crows. Juveniles were more hit-and-miss and often chose softer (less effective) surfaces, either through inexperience or because they were excluded from the better dropping zones. Crows hide shellfish for later consumption so that they have food for the times when their foraging places are covered by water.

21st Now, and over the next month, baby badgers are being born. The cubs are tiny, blind and helpless and will stay underground for around twelve weeks. Although a badger's pregnancy is short – around seven weeks – mating most likely took place many months ago, possibly last spring. Badgers are able to delay implantation into the uterus of the blastocyte, the pre-embryonic stage, until December. This means that when the cubs leave the sett in spring, the world is waking up, and it is a good time for finding food. They are partial to earthworms, but have a diverse diet, including the larvae of insects (bees, wasps, moths and craneflies) as well as slugs, frogs and vegetable matter. There are many old stories about badgers: one piece of fanciful folklore from County Sligo says 'there are two kinds of badger, the pig badger and the dog badger. The pig badger is big and wild looking. He would attack a person, but the dog badger is not so wild.' There are other tales of badgers throwing stones at humans, and even eating them.[i] In fact, badgers are more likely to scarper upon seeing a human.

22nd On mild winter days, the song thrush sings at dawn and dusk. His is a virtuoso performance: cascading coloratura trills and plaintive keening, interspersed with an outpouring of pips, chirrups and twitters. In the words of Robert Burns, 'aged Winter, 'mid his surly reign, / At thy blythe carol clears his furrowed brow'. The songsters are males establishing breeding territories. Each bird may have a repertoire of a hundred different phrases, often repeating one several times before moving on to the next. They leave short gaps during their renditions in order to listen for competition. The song thrush is a farmland and edge-of-woodland species, and its habitat is threatened by land drainage and tillage farming. It makes its nest in hedgerows and shrubs, and is equally happy in mature parks and gardens. In times past, thrushes were considered a friend to farmers and gardeners. An old verse, recorded in Donegal in the 1930s goes:

Don't kill the thrush, boys.
Don't rob its nest.
For of all the Irish warbles,
The brown bird is the best.

23rd Lesser celandine, a wild plant of woodland, hedgerows and gardens, is in bloom. It is a 'spring ephemeral', producing flowers and leaves only in the early part of the year. By summer these have died back, and the plant has vanished from sight. It maintains its presence underground in tuber form. The 'petals' on the buttercup-like flowers are not real petals, but are modified sepals, known as tepals. Their extreme glossiness, which is unusual among flowers, serves two distinct purposes. It sends a signal to distant pollinators by bouncing the sun's light, like the flash from a mirror. It also reflects heat onto the stamens and carpels (the reproductive structures) which helps pollen and seed to ripen – while also providing a warm spot for the pollinator. Lesser celandine was known colloquially as pilewort because the tubers were thought to resemble haemorrhoids. In folk medicine, the plant was used to cure that affliction, as well as pimples, ringworm and rottenness of the teeth and gums.

24th Bird lovers delight in seeing bullfinch families visiting feeders in winter. The males have jet black caps and portly bellies the crimson tone of an unwise holiday sunburn. The females are more demure, their black hats offset by muted, cappuccino-coloured breasts. Orchard owners are less enamoured of these stocky birds. When other food is scarce they systematically strip the buds from fruit trees, starting at the tips of branches and working inwards. Bullfinches can live for over twelve years, and recent research has strongly suggested that pairs stay together for multiple seasons – an assumption that has been made, but not proved, in the past. Olav Hogstad, an emeritus professor at the Norwegian University of Science and Technology, watched bullfinches for twenty-four years. He banded a total of 165 birds and found signs that pairs stay together through several winters, and therefore probably through several mating seasons. Long-term bonding such as this allows pairs to nest earlier in the year: they don't need to go through the annual hoopla of finding a mate.

25th Snowdrops are in flower. They are not part of our native flora, but they have naturalised and spread at a genteel rate in old estates, woodlands and churchyards. Most records are from Northern Ireland and counties Wexford, Waterford and Cork. The little white flowers – 'February's fair maids' – were traditionally associated with Candlemas Day, 2 February, and were a sign of purity and hope. They are flowering progressively earlier, however, and are now part of January's floral palette. The flowers open only on mild days, when pollinators are present to collect the nectar and the distinctive orange pollen. The eighteenth-century English poet Thomas Tickell, who lived in Dublin (in Glasnevin, on the property that later became the Botanic Gardens), dubbed the flowers 'vegetable snow' in his poem, 'Kensington Gardens'. In times past, snowdrops were sometimes planted to outline the way to the privy, which must have made a dark and chilly journey more bearable. During the Crimean war, officers sent bulbs home to Ireland of the local snowdrop (*Galanthus plicatus*), which then became the parent of various cultivated snowdrops. Some soldiers also planted them in 'gardens' around their tents. One, writing to his mother from the cavalry camp at Kadikoi, mentions that Lord Raglan, 'on seeing some *flowers* around a hut said, yes it was very well, but he should have had *cabbages* instead'.

26th Take a walk along any rocky shoreline and you'll see birds foraging among the seaweed-encrusted rocks. There is usually a heron fishing, while turnstone, herring gull and redshank rummage around, looking for molluscs and crustaceans among the strands of wrack. Oystercatchers, more often seen en masse on mudflats and sandy beaches, also frequent the rocky water's edge, stepping gingerly and inelegantly. Their awkwardly-toed feet seem ill-equipped for the uneven surface. An old Irish tale says that the oystercatcher lent its webbed feet to a gull, which never returned them. It seems also that it may have lent out its bill and received a cartoonish, bright orange carrot in return. Its beady, garnet eye and yin-yang, black-and-white plumage add to its comical looks. When it takes flight, however, with a 'pu-peep ... peep!', it is a dazzling, dynamic creature: all angular wings and vivid feather patterns.

27th In milder parts of the country, primroses are already popping out their pale flowers. Although they are the quintessential spring flowers of poets and romantics, they can be found in bloom any time from January into June. They provide valuable early nectar for a host of long-tongued insects, including bumblebees and bee-flies and the occasional butterfly emerging from hibernation. The primrose is also the larval food plant for at least four moths: silver-ground carpet, broad-bordered yellow underwing, double square-spot and green arches. Slugs and snails nibble its petals, while the foreign invader from southern Europe, the black vine weevil, will happily mash through the fleshy roots of garden populations. There is much traditional lore associated with the little yellow-flowered plants. They were used to cure a multitude of ailments, among them burns, cuts, piles, jaundice, tuberculosis, toothache and insomnia. In the farmyard, primroses were supposed to be efficacious in treating horse coughs and the sores on cows' udders.

28th The 'blue tit tweetles from the patio' now – to borrow an image from the Northern Irish poet, Michael Longley. The dapper male in his neat, blue-capped, bell-boy outfit sings brief melodies with a piccolo-like shrillness: high trills dropping quickly to lower notes. The female, who is nearby, is in similar plumage, but her blue hat, wings and tail are a little duller. Although blue tits raise only one brood during the year, they pair early and will begin to inspect nesting places soon. If you plan on putting up nest boxes (which they use readily), there is no time to be lost. Choose north- or northeast-facing walls or trees, two to four metres from the ground. Between seven and eleven eggs are laid and are timed to hatch during caterpillar season, from late April onwards. Both parents feed the nestlings. Blue tits can be long-lived: eleven years is the longest known lifespan. The greatest mortalities happen during the first season, with sparrowhawks and cats as the top predators.

29th Although February is frogspawn month for much of Ireland, January also sees a few precocious frogs engaged in the rigours of amplexus in sheltered ponds. Some may even breed in late December. When a female enters a pond, she is grabbed by a male (or two or three). Occasionally, if there are too many males, she may drown. As she releases her eggs, the male sheds sperm, fertilising them immediately. Each egg is enclosed in a capsule which swells in the water to form the familiar gelatinous globules. The jelly both protects and feeds the developing tadpoles, which take from ten to twenty-one days to hatch, depending on the weather. Often the first sign that frogs are about is the croaking of the males, a beckoning call to the females. 'Croaking' is an unfair description, as the sound is deep, resonant and regular: like a large woodpecker drumming on a hollow bamboo tube.

30th Walk along any relatively wild coastal stretch and you may see a robin-sized bird with black head, white half-collar and warm, russet waistcoat. It will be perched prominently on a fence post or shrub, and may allow you to get quite close before flitting off to another, slightly farther resting place. This is the stonechat, so named because its alarm call sounds like two smooth stones clacking together. The females are similar to the males (described above), but the colours are less contrasting, more washed out. During winter, birds on the coast are joined by those from bogs, heaths and rough slopes on higher ground. The oldest known *Saxicola rubicola* was found dead in Germany, having been ringed eight years and ten months previously. The species has several names in Irish. Among the most appealing are *Donncha an chaipín* (Donncha with the cap) and *Máirín an triúis* (Mary with the trousers) for the different sexes.

31st Today is the eve of Saint Brigid's Day or *Lá Fhéile Bhríde*, the feast of Ireland's female patron saint, a personage who morphed from pagan goddess to Christian divinity. Today (or tomorrow, at a pinch) is the time to gather rushes to make the characteristic Saint Brigid's cross, an emblem that may carry a legacy of solar symbolism. The crosses are made of sixteen pieces of soft rush (or *geataire* in Irish), and are believed to keep a home safe from misfortune. *Juncus effusus* is a common and familiar plant of marshes, roadsides, ditches, water edges and poorly drained pasture. In the mid-nineteenth century, David Bishop, curator of Belfast Botanic Gardens, discovered a peculiar, curling form of soft rush, *spiralis*, in Connemara. It is now sometimes grown as a curiosity by gardeners. Robert Lloyd Praeger, the Irish naturalist, later noted that the same form grew on various Atlantic islands off the west coast. The corkscrew rush has also been recorded in the Orkney Islands and the west of Scotland and Wales.

February

1st Today, according to some calendars, is the first day of spring. In Ireland, with our changeable weather, the season's start is a moveable feast. This month often brings snow. Equally, it may also bring warm sunshine – and everything else in between. In the past, the movements of hedgehogs were thought to predict the weather. Folklore collected in County Longford states: 'When the hedgehog comes out of his "nest" and sees his shadow on the 1st February, he goes back again for six weeks, because there's hard weather coming.' In fact, hedgehogs may wake on milder days and ramble around a bit, especially at the start or end of winter. In Donegal, the weather forecaster is a badger: if he appears on Candlemas Day (tomorrow) and sees his shadow, there will be bad weather for three months. In America, tomorrow is Groundhog Day, when the meteorological outlook depends on the prognosticating prowess of a groundhog, known also as a woodchuck.

2nd Shepherd's purse is in bloom now: it barely stops flowering all year. It is a wild plant of waste places and field margins. Its small, heart-shaped seed pods, which are delicately displayed on ankle-high stems, are more noticeable than the four-petalled, tiny, white flowers. It is the pods that give the plant its name, as they resemble the pouches worn by mediaeval peasants. When they split, minuscule golden seeds pour out, like Lilliputian coins. The seeds exude a glue when they become moist, and adhere to the feet of passing birds or animals, which then help to disperse them. In the doctrine of signatures, the pods were thought to resemble bladders and were used to treat urinary infections. *Capsella bursa-pastoris* belongs to the cabbage family (*Brassicaceae*) and is edible. If grown in fertile soil, the first leaves can be used as a baby-leaf salad, and the pods added to dishes for a peppery flavour. The garden carpet moth lays its eggs on shepherd's purse.

3rd This time of the year often sees unusual migrants arriving in Ireland. One such species is the glossy ibis, a dark and fantastical-looking, gothicky bird with stilts for legs and a sickle-shaped bill. At a distance the plumage is rook-black, but closer up, hints of iridescence become apparent. During the breeding season, these wading birds are a low-key maroon with shining wing coverts that show green, purple and amber highlights. The species originated in Africa, but since the nineteenth century its range has expanded to the Americas and Europe. The glossy ibis is a pioneer species, where some individuals are impelled to wander long distances prospecting for suitable new territories to colonise. Birds that turned up in County Wexford a few years ago had been ringed in Coto Doñana National Park in southern Spain. A pair nested and attempted to breed in Lincolnshire in 2014, but were unsuccessful. However, as our climate changes, it is probably only a matter of time before they establish here. You can check sightings of glossy ibis and other rare birds at irishbirding.com

4th Hazel catkins are swinging from twigs now, like the fingers of limp, mustard-yellow gloves. These are the male flowers, laden with masses of lightweight pollen which is then wafted by the breeze onto the tiny red-tasselled female flowers. Compared to insect carriers, which perform a door-to-door service, wind dispersal is an inefficient mechanism for moving pollen. Relatively huge amounts are released, with only a small portion finding its way to the female flowers. Hay fever sufferers may be affected by the tiny, airborne grains now. Bees collect hazel pollen for food, but they appear not to assist in fertilising the female flowers. These contain no nectar, so are of limited interest. In the Brehon Laws' hierarchy of trees, hazel was classified as a 'noble of the wood'.[ii] The trees were very valuable, both for their nuts and for their timber, which was used for furniture and fencing.

5th The 'household bird, with the red stomacher' as poet John Donne called the robin, is normally fiercely territorial outside the breeding season. Both males and females defend separate domains, singing and – if necessary – fighting to maintain their patches. However, during very harsh weather hostilities may be dropped in gardens where food is in plentiful supply. In late winter, females begin to prospect for partners, gingerly entering a male's zone. Cordial relations are gradually established, and for a few months birds will form harmonious pairs in order to breed and raise chicks. Nest building will commence in the coming weeks – an operation carried out entirely by the female. While she constructs the cup-shaped nest of dead leaves, moss, roots and hair, her mate feeds her, providing about a third of her daily intake. As she incubates the four to six eggs, he continues to bring her food. After about two weeks, the chicks hatch, and both parents feed them.

6th Keep your eyes on the ground, and sooner or later you'll see groundsel. The opportunistic little plant seeds into crevices in paving, along roadsides and in disturbed ground. It is immune to frost, and can be found in bloom any month of the year. It is not a thing of beauty, with its near-invisible, lemon-tipped, cylindrical flower heads and ragged leaves. *Senecio vulgaris* is closely related to the ragworts; the genus name comes from the Latin for old man, *senex*, which refers to the whiskery, white parachutes on the seeds. *Grúnlas* (in Irish) was frequently recommended as a folk remedy for many ailments, including jaundice, eczema, warts and distemper. In a poultice it was supposed to draw the corruption from a boil. Today, it is still fed to caged budgerigars and canaries.

It is the food plant for various moth caterpillars; it also provides a home for aphids. These, in turn, become food for other invertebrates and for small birds. Groundsel is an annual plant: germinating, growing and setting seed in the space of a year.

7th If you live in a suburban or greenish urban area, take a look at the surrounding chimneys and before too long you're bound to see a jackdaw. Often there is a pair. Members of the species mate for life and maintain the bond throughout the year. The jackdaw is the smallest of the dark crows and is easily recognised if you can get close enough. While much of the plumage is charcoal, the forehead and chin is jet black, as if the bird had dipped its face in a pot of ink. The eyes are disconcertingly pale and staring – like those of a goat. Jackdaws are cavity nesters, and researchers have posited that the white irises act as signals to fellow colony members that a particular niche is occupied. They remain faithful to the same nest year after year. This might be in a tree crevice, a cliff cranny, a fissure in a ruin, or even a rabbit hole. Occasionally you may see a bird with irregular white or pale splotches on its plumage. This is leucism, a condition where pigment is absent or diluted in some of the feathers. It is not uncommon in jackdaws.

8th There is a confusion of yellow dandelion-like flowers all year round. This month's special is coltsfoot, which sends up single flowers several weeks before the leaves. The ver-nacular name 'son-before-father' recognises this characteristic. The ray florets are finer and more lemony than those of dandelion. The stout, scale-covered flower stalks look touched with grey cobwebs, as do the large roundish leaves. These give the plant its name: they are supposed to resemble the hooves of a colt. The underside is coated with a fine, pale felt. In times past, this downy material was collected and used as tinder. Caleb Threlkeld, in his 1727 *Synopsis Stirpium Hibernicarum*, the first Irish flora, recommended boiling it in 'a Lixivium with a little salt-nitre' (lye and saltpetre) for the 'best Tinder'. The botanical name, *Tussilago farfara*, comes from the Latin *tussis*, a cough. The leaves were used as a cure for coughs, sometimes – not very helpfully – in tobacco form. Coltsfoot is still used in some herbal remedies.

9th Pied wagtails have roosted at night in Dublin's O'Connell Street for over ninety years. Robert Lloyd Praeger, in his classic book, *The Way that I Went* (1937), writes that they were first seen in the winter of 1929, in a tree 'that rose between sets of tramway rails, among bright arc lights, at a place where traffic is heavy and continuous'. Until the street's refurbishment at the beginning of this century, hundreds of birds (with a maximum of 3,600 in 1950) roosted in the plane trees from mid-October until mid-April. They still spend cold nights on O'Connell Street, but in much-diminished numbers. A newer roost has appeared outside the library on Dún Laoghaire's seafront. On the south west edge (opposite the upper entrance) is a large D-shaped water feature with a sunken bed of bamboos in the middle. A hundred or more wagtails roost in the greenery here, and for the next few weeks can be seen arriving at sunset. They gather on the roof of the library and drop down to the bamboos in twos and threes, like falling leaves.

10th How do earthworms fare in freezing weather? The temperature below the soil surface can be several degrees warmer than the air, so often it is business as usual there. When the soil temperature falls, our largest species, the common earthworm (*Lumbricus terrestris*), burrows deeper, as it cannot survive at temperatures lower than minus

1°C. Russian researchers found the species overwintering at depths of 1.5 metres. Its eggs are able to tolerate minus 5°C, through a mechanism whereby they automatically dehydrate in colder temperatures. When water freezes, it expands and causes damage, so the act of dehydration keeps the eggs safe. The tiger worm (*Eisenia fetida*), the species often found in wormeries, is unable to tolerate freezing temperatures, either in adult or egg form. It is not a soil-dwelling worm (preferring decomposing material) and is unable to escape the cold by tunnelling downwards. Another species, the octagonal-tailed worm (*Dendrobaena octaedra*), increases the amount of glucose – which acts as an antifreeze, a 'cryoprotectant' – in its body fluids.

11th As natural foods become depleted in the countryside, certain birds begin to appear at our garden feeders. Among them are siskins, small greeny-yellow finches that until now have been feeding on conifer, birch and alder seeds in forestry and woodlands. They are much daintier than their big, burly relatives, the greenfinches, and rarely weigh more than fifteen grams. Males have black skull-caps and splashes of bright yellow on wings, rump and face. Females are hatless and less boldly marked, with some streaking. They are acrobatic birds, often hanging upside down on feeders or the ends of branches in the same way as lesser redpolls. While some of these garden-visiting siskins are Irish in origin, some have come from Britain, Scandinavia and other parts of northern Europe. They can travel great distances: individuals ringed in Britain were subsequently found in Algeria, while a bird ringed in Mount Stewart in County Down was recaptured 1,892 kilometres away in Estonia.

12th In mild areas, three-cornered leek is already in bloom, although its main flowering period is from March onwards. It is one of our two common wild garlics, growing over much of Ireland, especially in a wide band along the east and south coasts. At a glance, *Allium triquetrum* could be mistaken for a white bluebell, but its floppy and inelegant triangular leaves and pungent, oniony smell identify it easily. It is naturalised, but not native. The species comes from the west and central Mediterranean, and was introduced to Britain and Ireland in the mid-eighteenth century. It has escaped again and again from the gardens where it was planted, sometimes in the form of discarded material. Over the last hundred years triangular-stalked garlic, as it is also known, has become well established in many habitats, especially along paths and smaller roads. As our climate warms, it is likely to spread farther. Its march across Ireland is aided by two advantages it holds over other plants. It flowers earlier and can therefore set and distribute seed sooner, and its bulbs are long-lived and can survive out of the ground for weeks. Early bees sometimes visit the flowers, while human foragers use all parts of the plant.

13th Although we may associate fungi with late summer and autumn, there are a few mushrooms that fruit in this season. The prettiest is the scarlet elf cup, a species that inhabits damp, broadleaf woodlands. It is so radiantly coloured and perfectly named that it might have stepped out of a children's book. It bears wide-mouthed goblets with smooth interiors of bright orange or red and with paler outsides that look as if they are coated in felt. The showy pigmentation and generous size (up to seven centimetres across) make scarlet elf cups easy to spot. *Sarcoscypha austriaca* grows on fallen, decomposing sticks, including alder, beech, cherry, hazel, willow and sycamore. It is usually found pushing through vibrantly green moss, making for a cheery colour combination. Appropriately, one of its other common names is moss cups. The concave surface and warm colouring of the cups help to concentrate the sun's rays in this chilly season, thus allowing the spores to ripen and disperse. The genus name comes from the Greek words *sarco* meaning flesh, and *skyphos*, a drinking vessel. The ruby elf cup (*S. coccinea*) is nearly identical: a positive identification of either species needs a microscope.

14th It is Saint Valentine's Day, so let's have a bit of shameless anthropomorphising. To the back-garden birdwatcher, few birds are as romantic as the collared doves, neatly dressed in their mocha-toned plumage and dark neck bands. They are almost always seen in couples, as they form long-lasting pair bonds. When perched, they sit closely together, quietly companionable, with none of the fidgeting of other birds. The song is a soothing 'coo-COO-coo', repeated again and again. Often you hear them before you see them: a flight call of a rasping 'kwaarrrr', accompanied by whistling wingbeats. Collared doves originated in India, but have spread westwards and, in the last century, rapidly. They first bred in England in 1955 and in Ireland in 1959. A pair produces three or more broods of one or two chicks per year. The nest is a sloppily built platform: the awkward, twiggy material is collected by the male and cobbled together by the female. Construction will commence shortly.

15th Alexanders is coming into flower in warmer parts, especially by the coast. Look for it along pathways and roadsides and under hedgerows. It is a substantial plant, immediately identifiable by its ornate, dark and shiny leaves. Before they flower, the bulky buds are wrapped inside a protective skin. It is an umbellifer, a plant with parasol-like arrangements of tiny flowers, the same family as cow parsley, hogweed, fennel, carrot, angelica and some thousands of other species. The Latin family name, *Apiaceae*, comes from *apium* for celery, which in turn comes from *apis* for bee. Flying insects of all kinds are attracted to the clan's accessible flowers. Alexanders is an archaeophyte: a plant that is not native to Ireland or Britain, but which was introduced before 1500. It was brought to Britain by the Romans, who used it as a spring tonic and vegetable. For centuries the entire plant was used, including the root and the young flower buds, which were pickled. It fell out of favour when celery became popular.

16th Wading birds that have overwintered in Ireland are already heading back north. We know this partly through the work of the Dublin Bay Birds Project, run by BirdWatch Ireland. The stretch of coastline between Sutton and Dún Laoghaire is one of the most important sites for wintering waterbirds, regularly supporting over thirty thousand birds of forty or more species. Since 2013, project members have been monitoring and colour-ringing birds. Re-sightings of the ringed individuals by dedicated birders reveal the birds' breeding places and the routes they take to get there. Some of the oystercatchers, for example, will stop off in the Inner Hebrides to breed, while others will travel on to Iceland before finding a mate. Birds flying to Iceland between now and mid-May include other waders (black-tailed godwits, golden plover, redshank, snipe and whimbrel), swans, geese, ducks, gulls and songbirds. They will return to

Ireland mainly in the autumn, but those that fail to breed may come back sooner, as early as the end of June.

17th Ivy plants are laden with round fruits that ripen from olive green to black. The leaves surrounding the berries are a simpler, more ovate shape than the angular and lobed leaf that we usually associate with ivy. The classic ivy leaf is found only on juvenile plants, the form that the species takes when it is clothing the ground or snaking up a wall or tree. When it reaches the top of the support, where there is more sunlight, the plant enters adulthood and is ready to reproduce. Its stems change to become thicker and self-supporting, the leaves take on a more oval profile and flowers begin to form. The berries are a nutritious food in this lean month. They are popular with many birds. The least elegant are the wood pigeons, who clumsily flap and tumble while gorging. Smaller, more delicate birds, such as blue tits, goldcrests and wrens, also bustle about in the ivy, searching deftly for the overwintering insects, eggs, larvae and spiders that are hidden there.

18th We're entering the season when male birds start throwing themselves around in the air with great bravado and vigour. These are courtship displays, a 'look at me!' to the females. They demonstrate speed, strength, agility and fitness: all qualities that any hen bird would like to see in the father of her chicks. The most spectacular (and perhaps the rarest) is the 'sky dancing' of the hen harrier, one of our most threatened bird species. The male flies higher and higher until he turns and falls to the ground, twisting, somersaulting and careering madly as he goes. Other birds perform less breathtaking aerobatics, but are just as determined. The wood pigeon flies steeply upwards, claps his wings over his back and glides downwards, tail spread into a fan. Wing-clapping is performed by all doves and pigeons. Many other birds provide aerial performances, including ravens, skylarks, blue tits, greenfinches, woodcock and lapwings. Even the house sparrow puts on a show, bouncing up and down, like a fluffy grey-and-brown yo-yo.

19th Feral goats are giving birth to their kids. Mating takes place between late summer and early winter and the young are born between January and early April. Some of our better-known wild herds are at Glendalough, Dalkey Island, the Burren and on Bilberry Rock in Waterford City. The last, a herd of about two dozen animals, are said to be the descendants of goats brought to Ireland at the end of the seventeenth century by Huguenot immigrants. They have thick and luxuriant coats, and may have Cashmere or Maltese ancestry. Most feral goats, however, are mixed breeds, and their genetic makeup may include the tall, white Swiss Saanen as well as the short, robust Old Irish. Goats were first introduced three or four thousand years ago by Neolithic farmers, who brought them into Antrim from Scotland. Goat hooves are split into two toes, each with hard outer sides and rubbery pads. This structure allows the feet to adjust minutely and continually to steep and uneven terrain.

20th The great spotted woodpecker is drumming on dead wood now, beating a rapid-fire tattoo that resonates across a wide area. The full-bodied reverberations, lasting just one or two seconds, announce his territorial rights over the region. Despite the 'great' appellation, this woodpecker is a relatively small bird: about the same length as a blackbird and a little slimmer. It is strongly marked in black and white with a red rear; males have an obvious red patch on the nape of the neck. The species has recently colonised Ireland from Britain, breeding in County Down in 2006 and in County Wicklow in 2008. It is still rare, but its range is spreading along the east coast, where individuals sometimes visit bird feeders close to woodland or forestry. Great spotted woodpeckers have tiny pockets of air behind their bills and strengthened bone tissues that prevent them suffering brain damage from drumming.

21st Elder is pushing bright green leaves from its buds already. It is the first native species to leaf up in spring, with some plants producing new foliage as early as January. Few people plant it these days; it is an unloved and underused species that falls somewhere between a straggly tree and an overgrown shrub. Nonetheless, it persists in hedgerows and plants itself in waste ground, and on roadsides, railway embankments and woodland edges. The foliage has an unpleasant odour when bruised and is supposed to be unpalatable to browsing animals. In the past, bunches were tied to horses' harnesses to keep flies away. Elder has countless culinary, medicinal and practical uses. Berries and flowers can be made into wine and 'champagne'. Traditionally, the hollowed stems were used by children to make pea shooters and water pistols. In Longford, stems were filled with molten lead to make 'a good weapon for protection on a journey or out walking at night' according to Roy Vickery's *Oxford Dictionary of Plant-Lore*. Elder is a short-lived species, often lasting only two or three decades. The young wood is soft and easily compressed, like vegetable polystyrene. The pith was once widely used in labs (and biology class) as a holding material when slicing cell-thin cross-sections of specimens for microscope slides. Pieces of pith are still sold by some laboratory supply companies.

22nd Pairs of magpies have started to build new nests and refurbish old ones in the tops of large trees. Existing nests may have been used as winter roosting places by other birds, such as hooded crows. There may be angry arguments as the rightful owners regain possession. In urban areas, magpies occasionally build nests on streetlights or electrical poles. The construction process can go on in a desultory way for weeks. Usually, the male forages for material and brings it to the female, flying determinedly in an arrow-straight path to the nest. Building material can be large and awkward, and includes long sticks, lengthier than the bird. The nest is a tall dome lined with grass, hair or fine roots and held together with mud. Five or six eggs are laid in April, and are incubated by the female. After less than three weeks the chicks hatch, and are fed by both parents. Magpies usually live about five years. The oldest recorded individual was ringed as a nestling in Coventry in 1925 and shot in 1947 at 21 years, 8 months and 23 days.

23rd It's important to keep bird feeders topped up now, as many of the foods provided by nature are running out. Most plants, both cultivated and wild, have exhausted their berries or seeds. A few stragglers still offer pickings to small birds: the seedheads of artichokes, cardoons and mulleins are eagerly inspected for stray seeds and for the invertebrates sheltering in the dry depths. Teasel continues to attract goldfinches. Adult aphids may overwinter on plants, especially evergreen ones, where they are shielded from the worst of the elements. They are generally females, and when the weather warms up, they give birth to more aphids. On certain trees, including maple, sycamore, chestnut and various fruit trees, there are little clusters of aphid eggs around the buds. They are timed to hatch just as the buds start to unfold in spring. All these morsels of protein – the adults, the eggs and the hatchlings – provide vital nutrition for birds during this period of slim pickings.

24th White-tailed eagles are courting, soaring in pairs above their eyries. The wingspan can be up to 2.4 metres, making them, along with mute swans, our 'wingspanniest' bird. An average human with outstretched arms falls well short of this. Sea eagles, as they are also called, were once widespread around our coast, but by the beginning of the twentieth century poisoning and shooting had wiped them out. Victorian collectors seeking eggs and skins also hastened the demise of these majestic raptors. Between 2007 and 2011, a hundred birds were reintroduced to Killarney National Park. The young birds came from wild nests in Norway. In the eagle world when two chicks are hatched, the second rarely survives, so these are the birds that are used in reintroduction programmes. By the end of 2019, Ireland's new white-tailed eagles had raised twenty-seven young, in territories from the Beara Peninsula to Connemara. Over the coming weeks, eggs will be laid, incubated, and – it is hoped – more eaglets fledged. Sea eagles are mainly scavengers, eating dead fish and mammals. They also steal from other predators; sometimes they catch their own prey, swooping dramatically to the water to grab an unwary fish.

25th The ground in parks and gardens that was bare in winter is covered in a green haze of seedling leaves. Some of our most persistent wild plants – or weeds, to gardeners – are annuals. They die in autumn and appear anew each spring, sprouting from seeds in the soil. Cleavers (vernacularly known as sticky-backs and many other names) is one of the first to germinate. Some of its seeds bounced off the parent plant last year and are now starting new populations on the home ground. Others stuck to the fur of animals and clothes of humans, and were carried far from their origins. Chickweed, another common annual, is also enjoyed by domestic fowl – and budgerigars. It is springing up all over vegetable patches and flower beds. Ivy-leaved speedwell is also proliferating. The first leaves are neat ovals; they are followed by miniature, ivy-shaped true leaves, covered in hairs. In some ditches the leaves of wild arum are appearing, like sheaves of glossy arrowheads.

26th Bramblings are with us now, pretty finches visiting from Scandinavia and farther east. They are the same size and weight as chaffinches, but the plumage is bolder. At this time of the year, males have blackish-brown heads, rusty breasts and white bellies and rumps. Backs and wings are a scatter of brown, rust and white, like burnt toast that has been hastily scraped. Females are similar but more muted. In both sexes, the snowy rumps are noticeable when birds are in flight. Single birds, or twos and threes, may visit gardens and bird feeders – along with other finches, especially chaffinches. But they are more likely to congregate where there are beech trees; beech mast is their preferred food. In previous years flocks have gathered at Powerscourt House in Enniskerry in County Wicklow and at Curraghchase Forest Park in County Limerick, among other places. In late March, bramblings head home for the breeding season where they build nests in birch woodlands or on the edges of mixed conifer and birch forests.

27th Winter cherry (*Prunus subhirtella* 'Autumnalis') has been in flower since November or earlier. In colder years it takes a break in January and February and sets off again with a fresh blast of blossom in March and April. It is a Japanese variety, but it was introduced to western gardens by a famous Irish nursery in County Down. In 1901, Tom Smith of Daisy Hill Nursery received the first specimens in Europe in a consignment of plants from Japan. For many years this cherry was a rarity, as it must be propagated from cuttings or grafted onto the rootstock of another cherry. The pale pink, delicate blossom is visited by winter-foraging bumblebees.

It never bears fruit. A related tree, also in flower now, is the cherry-plum (*Prunus cerasifera*), a native of southern Europe and western Asia that has been growing here for centuries. It is often used as a hedgerow plant. The white flowers with their prominent stamens are similar to those of blackthorn, but they appear some weeks earlier, and the branches are thornless. A pink-flowered form has wine-toned leaves. Both are good early bee plants. Small fruits are sometimes borne in late summer.

28th Buff-tailed bumblebee queens – and workers, in mild areas – have been around all winter. Young queens of other species are beginning to emerge from hibernation. Each one mated last summer and stored the sperm inside her body. As soon as she wakes in early spring, she seeks out flowers such as deadnettle, winter heather, lesser celandine, crocus and rosemary. She needs pollen and nectar to restore her body fats and develop her ovaries. If you see a large bee buzzing along at ground level rather than visiting flowers, it is a queen looking for somewhere to make her nest. This may be an old mouse hole, a deep crevice in a wall or the hollow space at the base of a plant or clump of grass. When she finds her ideal spot, she may rearrange leaves and other debris for insulation. Before laying eggs, she makes a wax pot and fills it with nectar, to supply her with sustenance during the incubation period. She lays her eggs on top of a ball of pollen and keeps them warm under her furry abdomen until they hatch.

29th As winter progresses, the leafier, softer parts of seaweed scattered on the beach are worn away by the action of waves against sand and pebble. The stipes (stems) of kelp are more durable and remain strewn about like rubbery brown sticks. At the base of some, the holdfast remains, a formation like a many-fingered fist. The fingers, known as haptera, colonise microscopic crevices on rock surfaces underwater and secrete a waterproof glue. This keeps the seaweed securely fastened in place through months or years of continual movement. The space within the haptera offers a habitat to dozens of tiny creatures, including crustaceans, tubeworms and molluscs. It is worth looking closely at the fresher holdfasts you find on the beach to see what is living within the space enclosed by the haptera. One resident is the blue-rayed limpet, a small shell (less than two centimetres) with shimmering turquoise bands painted across its domed surface. It carves out a niche in the seaweed's fabric that can weaken the holdfast's bond, causing it to become dislodged and washed ashore.

March

1st It is Saint David's day, the patron saint of Wales. The sixth-century Welsh bishop is also revered in parts of Ireland: there is a holy well dedicated to him at Ballynaslaney in County Wexford. David's emblem is the leek. In the Irish flora, the nearest thing is Babington's leek (*Allium babingtonii*), a plant that may be an archaeophyte – a relict of cultivation prior to 1500 CE. It is perennial, growing wild in sandy and poorish soil. It is most frequent along the west coast, from southwest Clare to south Donegal; there are also numerous records of it in County Wexford. It is locally common on the Aran Islands where it was used in the same way as garlic. The strappy new leaves have been coming up for some weeks. By the time the plant blooms in late summer (on stems that may be nearly two metres), the foliage has withered and disappeared. The flower heads are a mix of tiny mauve florets and tightly packed bulbils. In traditional veterinary medicine, blackleg, a disease of cattle, was supposed to be cured by putting half a bulbil into a slit in a calf's tail. The plant was named after an English botanist and archaeologist, Charles Cardale Babington, by his friend and fellow botanist, William Borrer.

2nd Although it may look like spring in some parts of Ireland, it's important to keep feeding the birds. Last year's wild crop of seeds, fruits and nuts is almost spent, and this season's first generation of insects is barely getting started. Small birds can lose 20 per cent of their body weight keeping warm on a harsh night: they need to eat constantly during daylight if they are to survive. Garden feeding stations with energy-rich seeds, sunflower hearts and suet are life savers.

Blackcaps and other territorial species may protect some food sources and drive off all comers, so more birds have a chance if there are several feeders. Snow sometimes hits in March or April; food should definitely be supplied then. Birds also require water to avoid dehydration. Eating snow is not a realistic option as melting it saps a huge amount of a bird's energy. During cold snaps in Europe, continental birds such as redwings, fieldfares and waxwings come to Ireland looking for sustenance, and may visit gardens.

3rd Some biennial plants (those that flower in their second year of growth) spend the winter as rosettes: neat ground-hugging clusters of leaves. One of the most common is mullein, with its unmistakable clumps of grey-green, felted leaves. In early morning the furry surfaces are silvered with tiny dew drops. While this effect looks pretty to our eyes, it is a mechanism that many rosette-formers use to collect moisture. Other such plants are foxglove, spear thistle, marsh thistle, teasel and weld or dyer's rocket. All these biennials need 'vernalisation' in order to recommence growth in spring. This means that their systems require a period of cold before they can respond to stimuli such as lengthening days and rising temperatures. The cold triggers the plant to switch from a vegetative mode (growing leaves) to a reproductive one (producing flowers). As spring advances, flower stems will begin to emerge from the rosettes, lengthening gradually until they bloom.

4th Song thrushes, robins, blackbirds and sparrows are in full voice. Blue tits are singing too, mostly variations of a chirrupy 'chee-chee-purrrr-ah'. In woodlands, the dominant proclaimer this month is the great tit. Its most common declaration is a ringing, far-reaching, high-low refrain: 'Teacher! teach-er! teach-er!' It also sounds like a vastly amplified squeaky wheelbarrow. This basic phrase is often reworked and embroidered with grace notes. Seventy different utterances, including alarm calls and songs, have been identified among great tits, with each bird normally having a repertoire of about eight songs. When a male is defending his territory, he uses different songs in different areas to fool potential intruders into thinking they are facing multiple birds instead of a lone, resourceful individual. The great tit is the largest of its family to visit gardens. Weighing eighteen grams, it is considerably bulkier than the coal tit or blue tit. It has a black head with white cheeks, a yellow breast and an olive-green back. It also sports a vertical black chest stripe. Males with the widest stripes are most attractive to females.

5th Wheels of jagged dandelion leaves have been expanding since the start of the year, pressed flat against the ground. In milder areas their spring flush of flower is beginning. Within a month their cheery yellow heads will cover grassy verges and weedkiller-less lawns. Some will host pollen beetles, tiny, shiny, black or greeny-bronze insects that tumble about among the petals. Each flower is a composite of individual florets (sometimes over two hundred) with each having a reservoir of nectar and a dusting of pollen. This makes them an important source of food for early bumblebees, honeybees, solitary bees, hoverflies, butterflies and other insects. About a dozen moth species lay their eggs on the plants, which then feed the caterpillars. Later, when the clocks form, goldfinches and house sparrows pluck the seeds. There is no definitive dandelion species. Instead, there is an aggregate of hundreds of microspecies: over seventy different forms have been identified in Dublin alone. Look carefully at a few dandelions in the coming weeks, and you will see how they differ in leaf shape and coloration. Many other factors vary, but these are the easiest to spot.

6th Seabirds are putting on their breeding plumage, which makes them easier to identify. A small but striking bird is the black guillemot, which is a deep sooty brown (nearly black), with a well-defined white wing patch. The legs and inside of the mouth are a rich coral red. It is an auk, a family that includes guillemot, puffin and razorbill. Black guillemots are found all along the coast and are easily spotted in the relatively calm water of various harbours, including Bangor, Dingle, Dún Laoghaire and Howth. The birds float quietly, most often in ones and twos, and disappear from view periodically, as they dive for small crustaceans and fish. Occasionally a small group flies low and fast over the waves. The species' diminutive size and habit of nesting in crevices and holes in walls led to its common names in Ireland of sea pigeon and rock dove (not to be confused with the European rock dove, mentioned on 16 January). In Roundstone in County Galway, a vernacular name was 'parrot', according to the Reverend Charles Swainson's 1885 book, *The Provincial Names and Folklore of British Birds*. Britain and Ireland are the black guillemot's southernmost breeding range. It breeds as far north as Greenland and Alaska.

7th Butterbur is in flower in milder areas. *Petasites hybridus* is like a better-looking, jumbo version of its invasive relative, winter heliotrope (*P. fragrans*). Growing along rivers, damp roadsides and other moist places, it carries batons of pink-tipped, tasselled, tubular flowers, thirty to forty centimetres tall. The round and scalloped leaves, emerging now, can expand to ninety centimetres when fully grown. They are also soft and flexible, and were used for wrapping butter in the days before refrigeration. Almost all instances in Ireland are male, so the species can spread to new territories only by the roots fragmenting and starting new plants. In David Moore's 1866 flora of Ireland, *Cybele Hibernica*, butterbur was recorded predominantly around houses and gardens in some regions, suggesting that, although native, some populations are relicts of cultivation. In some countries, a preparation known as Ze339, made from an extract of the leaves, is used to alleviate the symptoms of allergic rhinitis. Research has also shown an extract of the root to be effective in reducing the frequency of migraines.

8th If you take a holiday in a warmer climate during this season, you may notice plenty of birdsong. Sometimes the singers are familiar birds, but the melody and timbre may be slightly different. A Canary Island blackbird, for example, gives a less liquid and more staccato performance than its Irish counterpart. Birdsong can vary from region to region, especially in non-migratory species. Even on a small geographic scale, birds of the same species may have distinct 'dialects'. This happens when colonies are separated by a mountain, water or other inhospitable terrain. Dialects are learned, with young birds adopting the local versions sung by the neighbourhood males. Females usually respond to males vocalising in their own dialect. With some species, however, they may choose males with different dialects, perhaps to widen the genetic base of the next generation. City birds, meanwhile, may sing at higher frequencies than their country cousins: this allows their voices to be heard above the urban din.

9th The summer snowflake is misnamed, as its flowering period – just starting – is over and done with in May. The lampshade-like flowers on this bulb are roughly similar to those of snowdrops, but they dangle in small groups of three to six on tall, knee-high stalks. There are six identical petals, instead of the snowdrop's arrangement of three outer and three inner petals. Each white petal is tipped with a lime-green nub. *Leucojum aestivum* is rare in the wild in Ireland, and only a portion of the population – along the banks of the Shannon and in the southeast – is believed to be native. The other instances are probably garden plants that have jumped into the wider countryside, possibly by seeds travelling along watercourses. The fruits are inflated with air, which allows them to float. Leucojum establishes in moist places such as riversides, marshes and damp meadows. There are large colonies at Inistioge in Kilkenny and Innishannon in Cork.

10th Some garden ponds, ditches and bog pools are wriggling with little black tadpoles. Others are still hosting clumps of gelatinous frogspawn in various stages of development, from the solid black pinheads of eggs to the elongating commas of embryonic tadpoles. Prolonged spells of freezing weather, such as those that sometimes hit this month, can kill off both the eggs and the budding tadpoles. Eggs on the bottom of clumps may survive, if they are floating in unfrozen water. Free-swimming tadpoles may also live, provided that the pond is not sealed with ice long enough to become anoxic (deprived of oxygen). Individual frogs lay only one batch of spawn per year, so the producers of frost-damaged eggs will have no progeny this spring. However, some frogs spawn late, so even in very cold years, there will be tadpoles somewhere. If your pond freezes, place a pan of hot water on top of it, to melt a hole in the ice. Sometimes, floating a ball on the surface prevents the water from freezing overnight.

11th Let us consider the 'Lent lilies', as daffodils are sometimes known. In Irish it is *lus an chromchinn*, the plant with the bowed head. Although it is not native in Ireland, several different daffodil species and hybrids have become naturalised, forming colonies in demesnes and gardens and around old ruins. Some communities are very old: a planting of the scented *Narcissus* x *medioluteus* on Killiney Hill in County Dublin has been known for over two centuries – although the increased volume of foot traffic now means that its days are probably numbered. Daffodils are an important forage plant for early bees and other pollinators. Another insect depending on daffodils and other bulbs is the large narcissus fly (*Merodon equestris*) – much despised by bulb growers. This furry hoverfly, which mimics a small bumblebee, is a harmless consumer of nectar and pollen when an adult. Its immature phase is another matter. The larva hatches from a single egg laid at the neck of the bulb in May or June. It tunnels into the bulb's interior and chomps through the tissues, spending months steadily munching away and leaving behind its excretions of gooey, brown frass. In early spring, the larva moves to the adjoining soil, pupates for a few weeks and then emerges as an innocent hoverfly.

12th In its winter plumage the great crested grebe is an almost puritanical-looking bird, quietly dressed in grey, white and buff. Its dark head plumes, however, jauntily backswept into a quiff, are a hint of the glories that appear now in the breeding season. In spring, the body plumage becomes more richly coloured, and the head and neck are adorned with a double-tufted black crest and chestnut ruff. The birds' famous courtship display takes place on the lakes, reservoirs and quiet waterways where they will build their nests. With crest and ruff spread tall and wide, a pair dances on the water in a synchronised performance that oscillates between gracefully balletic and energetically slapstick. They head-shake, preen, dip, rise up, tread water, dive and offer each other gifts of waterweed. The nest is a floating platform tethered to vegetation, so that it doesn't drift away. Demand for the birds' plumage in Victorian times nearly wiped out the British and Irish populations. By 1860 there were around fifty pairs in Britain. The finely feathered chest skins, known as 'grebe fur', were used in clothing, while the head plumes were added to hats.

13th Wood anemones, or wooden enemies, as wits are wont to call them, are in bloom now. Their starry white flowers speckle the ground in mature woodlands and in undisturbed areas in older estates and gardens. Large gatherings are indicators of very old woodland, as the plant spreads at a painfully slow pace, mostly via thin, underground rhizomes, rather than by seed. Clumps are reputed to increase by no more than six feet per hundred years. During rainy or dull weather and at night time, the flowers close up and hang downwards, like minuscule white handkerchiefs. In sunshine they open wide, revealing exquisitely poised golden stamens. Hoverflies and occasionally honeybees visit them. *Anemone nemorosa* is a spring ephemeral: after flowering, the leaves die back. The plant completely disappears for the rest of the year, its place taken by ferns and mosses. The wood anemone belongs to the same family as the buttercup. Imagine the flowers as yellow instead of white, and the resemblance is clear.

14th Mad March hares are boxing now. They stand on hind legs, batting at each other in quick-fire bouts of frantic, speedy energy. The sparring pairs are usually a female and male, with the former fighting off the attentions of the latter. The bucks are a little smaller than the does: it is possible that the clash is also a test of his strength and stamina. She is more likely to choose a fit and feisty father for her offspring. Our native hare, *Lepus timidus hibernicus*, is endemic to Ireland (that is, occurring nowhere else) and is a subspecies of the white Arctic hare. Unlike the northern species, the Irish hare does not turn white in winter. Its coat may be anywhere between light brown and dark russet, tones that blend well into our countryside. The Irish hare is found all over our island, from upland bogs to sea level dunes. The greatest numbers are on grassland, such as farmland, golf courses and airfields – including Dublin Airport. The busiest mating season is spring and summer, but breeding can happen all year round. The longer-limbed and longer-eared European brown hare (*L. europaeus*) has been introduced here several times since the nineteenth century; the two species sometimes crossbreed.

15th Leaves are emerging on some trees, while others are bare. Still others are carrying sere remnants of last year's foliage, fruits and seeds. Old relics are just as much a part of the tree-scape at this time of the year as new growth. Young beech, oak and hornbeam hold on to their rustling brown leaves until well into spring. Ash is still untidy with bundles of 'keys' (seeds): it is the last to leaf up and may be stark and skeletal for many more weeks. Plane trees are adorned with the occasional knobbly seed ball, while on rowan and crab apples a few dried fruits hang – those that escaped the attentions of birds. The great hand-like leaves of horse chestnut are squeezing out of the sticky buds, like lime-green crumpled gloves. In gardens and parks, purple-leaved cherry-plum has been in leaf for over a month and is still sporting dainty pink flowers. On river banks, cascading weeping willows are hazed with green.

16th Sand martins are the smallest of the hirundines that breed here in summer. The others, which share the characteristic bullet body, forked tail and swept-back wings, are barn swallows and house martins. The brown-and-white sand martins are the earliest to arrive, with the first small parties flying in around now. They have spent the winter in Africa, just below the Sahara in the semi-arid Sahel zone. They are faithful to breeding sites, returning year after year to the same locations, which may host colonies of hundreds of birds. Older individuals may return two or three weeks before first-year birds. While this ensures that they can be among the first to set up house in the side of a cliff or quarry, it also puts them at risk from cold March weather. In the coming weeks, pairs will be excavating burrows and lining them with grass and feathers. Despite their petite size, sand martins are adept at digging, shifting heavy stones and other material.

17th There is no true shamrock. Historically, five different trifoliate plants have done service as Saint Patrick's emblem on this day. The species that is grown commercially is yellow clover (*Trifolium dubium*), also known as lesser trefoil. It blooms from May onwards with tiny, canary-coloured tuft-like flowers. Its leaves provide food for caterpillars of the common blue butterfly. White clover was another of the shamrocks. In 1726, Caleb Threlkeld notes in his Irish flora:

This Plant is worn by the People in their Hats upon the 17. Day of March yearly, (which is called St. Patrick's Day.) It being a Current Tradition, that by this Three Leafed Grass, he emblematically set forth to them the Mystery of the Holy Trinity. However that be, when they wet their Seamar-oge, they often commit Excess in Liquor, which is not a right keeping of a Day to the Lord; Error generally leading to Debauchery.

Other plants once used as shamrocks were red clover, black medick and wood sorrel.

18th The wren is the loudest bird in the garden now, declaiming in five-second bursts of clear, trilling sound that end abruptly as if an 'off' button has been pressed. The song is both to defend territory from other males and to attract a mate. Despite its great volume, the wren can be difficult to spot, as it is most often surrounded by dense vegetation. Its short, rounded wings are adapted to life in this congested habitat. They allow take-off and other manoeuvres to be accomplished speedily in cramped conditions. Each male builds several nests in his territory ('cock nests') and when a female shows interest, he escorts her around his various bits of real estate. One of her criteria is a secluded location, well hidden from potential predators. If she finds a nest that she likes, she adds the finishing touches, bringing in hair and feathers to soften and insulate it. Some males are polygamous, especially in areas where there is abundant food. When they have settled one female in a nest they go off in search of more mates.

19th Moths get bad press, thanks to a few rogues such as the common clothes moth and the codling moth, which is fond of apples. However, of the 1,500-plus species native to Ireland, most do no damage to fabric or food. Some act as pollinators and many provide sustenance to birds and bats and other mammals. Blue tits are just one of the birds that time their broods to coincide with caterpillar season. Several macro-moths – those that are larger and thus easier to identify – are on the wing already. Among these is the beautifully marked emperor (*Saturnia pavonia*), which belongs to the same family as the silkworm. Males are mostly russet-coloured, while females, which are larger, are more sepia-toned. Both have eye-spots on all four wings, and are decorative enough to be mistaken for a butterfly. Look for them in open, scrubby ground and in hedgerows near brambles, heather and hawthorn – some of the plants fed on by the caterpillars. See mothsireland.com for help with identifying the moths that you find.

20th Cherry laurel is in bloom, holding up slim torches of creamy flower amid large, shiny, leathery leaves. In the past, this native of eastern Europe and southwest Asia was planted extensively on estates for game cover and beautification. By the mid-twentieth century, those well-intended plantings were choking demesne woodlands with evergreen thickets. They marched along, relentlessly sending up new shoots from the base and forming roots where branches touched the ground (processes known as suckering and layering). Bird-dispersed fruits also allowed the plants to jump into the wild. Laurel is now considered an invasive species of high impact, as it shades out native plants and degrades habitats. For non-botanists, it's hard to believe that this elephantine shrub, with its thick leaves and batons of blossom, is a cherry, but its Latin name, *Prunus laurocerasus*, signifies its membership of the *Prunus* or cherry genus. Despite its general undesirability in the wild, it is popular with bees, hoverflies and butterflies, as it produces plenty of nectar. This comes not just from its flowers, but also from nectar-secreting glands (known as extrafloral nectaries) on the undersides of the leaves.

21st Cock pheasants are looking their pompous best for the breeding season. They strut regally with magnificent tails, gleaming blue-green necks, bright-red faces and dazzling white collars. Body and wing plumage is a sumptuous mix of russets and brown with white and dark markings. Males gather a bevy of females, in the same manner as domestic chickens – both belong to the *Galliformes* order of birds. Pheasants fly only short distances, but they roost in trees at night, out of harm's way. The hens lay their eggs on the ground in shallow dips, sometimes in the shelter of a bramble or hedgerow. They are not a native species, and are originally from Asia. All those that we see now on roadsides and in parks and woodlands are escapees from shoots, or their descendants. The Romans probably introduced the bird to Britain, but the earliest records in Ireland date from around the sixteenth century.

22nd We have over a dozen native and naturalised species of willow, as well as an array of hybrids. Osiers were often planted in hedgerows and close to houses to provide material for baskets and wickerwork. Such plantings were known as sally gardens: the name is a derivation of the Latin species name, *Salix*. Most willows are blooming now, although the catkins, as they are known, don't look like normal flowers. Immature male catkins – pussy willows – are covered in grey fur, which acts as insulation during cold weather. As they mature, they elongate, the stamens protrude, and the copious yellow pollen on the anthers is visible. Willows are wind-pollinated, but they are also visited by bees, which stock up on pollen. Nectar is sometimes produced, and this is a life-saving boost for butterflies emerging from hibernation. The smallest species is the creeping willow, which rarely tops a metre. It grows most often near the coast, on sandy and rocky ground. Look for silvery or silky leaves and little catkins.

23rd Hibernating butterflies sometimes rouse on warm and sunny winter days, but after soaking in a few rays they return to their slumbers. Sunny March days, however, cause surges of butterflies to properly wake up and fly off in search of mates. Peacock, small tortoiseshell, brimstone, comma and red admiral butterflies all overwinter in adult form. The last two have begun to hibernate here only in recent years. Painted lady also attempts to hibernate here, but may not survive. In mild areas the very first of the season's freshly hatched holly blues may be on the wing. These tiny, pale and luminous butterflies are easy to miss, as they dance in the air some metres overhead and barely stay still. They overwintered as chrysalises on the undersides of the leaves of ivy and various other plants, including bramble. Early summer will see a wave of migrants, including painted lady, red admiral and comma, arriving from abroad.

24th The first of our native hedgerow plants to flower is blackthorn. Its clouds of white blossom billow out from roadside and motorway plantings. The impenetrable thickets of dark twigs – with each shoot ending in a vicious spine – give shelter to the nests of birds, including wrens, blackbirds, thrushes, tits and finches. The leaves provide food for the caterpillars of over fifty different moths. The brown hairstreak butterfly also lays its eggs on blackthorn. The butterfly, which is a rich, rusty orange rather than the brown of its name, is confined to the Burren and a few other places. In autumn, the tremendously bitter sloes, which look like miniature plums, will be eaten by birds and foraged by humans for sloe gin and hedgerow jelly. The stones from sloes picked over a thousand years ago were found in excavations of Viking Dublin. More recently, other parts of the plant were made into folk remedies, while the dried leaves were used as a tobacco substitute. The best-known uses of the wood are for walking sticks and, in the past, for fighting sticks. After the stick was cut it was seasoned in the smoke of the chimney.

25th The dunnock, also known as the hedge sparrow, is a small brown bird. It is not related to the house sparrow, but from a distance it looks similar. It has a slimmer, more pointed bill and more uniform colouring. The dunnock's manner is careful and diffident, as it shuffles around in the undergrowth, nearly invisible in its sensible, mousy outfit. The Irish-born Victorian ornithologist, the Reverend Frederick Orpen Morris, advocated it as a role model for humans: 'unobtrusive, quiet and retiring … humble and homely in its deportment and habits, sober and unpretending in its dress…' Morris was magnificently wrong, for the dunnock's sex life is so intense that the good reverend is no doubt spinning and blushing in his grave. While a few individuals are monogamous, most dunnocks make complex liaisons involving one, two or even three members of the opposite sex. A ménage à trois of two males and one female is the most common. During the ten-day mating period, starting soon, polyandrous females copulate on average 1.6 times an hour. Females solicit more than one mate because each male who shares paternity of the brood helps to feed her chicks.

26th Young fox cubs are nestled in their dens. In urban areas, vixens may set up house under tool sheds or decking or in an overgrown garden or ruined building. Most cubs are born in March, in litters of four or five. The cubs' coats are brown when they are first born, and their eyes – which turn a glowing amber as they get older – are blue. Both parents hunt for their offspring, while unmated females born the previous year also often help with care. Rats, mice, nestlings, birds' eggs and roadkill are all brought back to the den. Back-garden poultry, where available, is a delicacy. The cubs will emerge in the coming weeks, at first staying near the entrance of the den. Later they will play in the open, often stealing balls, plastic plant pots and other items. By the end of the summer they will be able to hunt and forage for themselves.

27th Barn swallows are returning to Ireland. The first few individuals have been flying in from their wintering grounds in southern Africa over the last couple of weeks. These are most likely males, who arrive before the females to establish a nest site. Birds remain faithful to the same nest places from year to year, building their mud and straw cups up against the beams inside barns and sheds. Swallows can be distinguished from their cousins, the martins, by their high-low, swooping, gliding flight and their lengthy, deeply forked tails. Females' tails are a little shorter. Males with the longest, most symmetrical tail streamers are the most sought after. Swallows often gather communally on wires, nattering constantly in lightweight, liquid voices. They will raise two or even three broods of young before returning south for the winter. Swallows feed entirely on insects, favouring larger flies such as horseflies and bluebottles. Their food supply suffers where pesticides are used, including animal worming medications. Such drugs render cowpats sterile, so that flies' eggs don't hatch on them.

28th Solitary bees are emerging from their nests and are feeding on dandelion and willow flowers. Unlike honeybees or bumblebees, they do not form cooperative communities. Instead, the young raise themselves, having been provided with the equivalent of a packed lunch by their mother. After mating in late spring or summer, she searches for a suitable nest site. This might be in an earthen bank, a crack in masonry, or even a manmade 'bee hotel', depending on her species. She collects pollen, makes it into a cake and lays a single egg on it. She repeats the process – one cake, one egg – until her eggs are finished, after which she dies. The larvae hatch, feed on the pollen and overwinter in cocoons. In spring they emerge as adults and the cycle starts again. A few species are 'kleptoparasites', laying eggs in the nests of other solitary bees. Most of our seventy-seven solitary bee species are smaller than a honeybee. Some are very efficient pollinators. They carry pollen on the underside of the abdomen, instead of on the legs: with each flower visit, pollen is left behind. The red mason bee (*Osmia bicornis*), which readily uses bee hotels, can provide 120 times the pollinating services of a honeybee.

29th Violets are in flower. We have several species, but the common dog violet (*Viola riviniana*) is by far the most widespread – in woodlands, banks, hedgerows and pastures. The 'dog' denotes that it has no scent, unlike the sweet violet. In parts of Britain, 'horse' and 'pig' replace the dog. Its pale purple flowers are borne singly and the leaves are hairless and heart-shaped. You can tell it apart from the similar early dog violet (*V. reichenbachiana*) because its spur (the tiny finger at the back of the flower) is pale, instead of dark. Or maybe you can't: the two species have intermingled, especially in Leinster, and it can be hard to put a name on some plants. Violets have multiple interactions with insects. The flowers provide valuable early forage for bees, while the caterpillars of certain fritillary butterflies feed on the foliage.

Violet seeds have a fatty appendage, called an elaiosome. This attracts ants, which unwittingly disperse them by transporting them to their nests. After the elaiosome is eaten, the seed is removed to a 'rubbish' area, where other organic matter makes the soil more fertile. The seedlings from these natural compost heaps have larger leaves than others.

30th The first basking sharks of the year are appearing off the coast of Ireland. Between now and late autumn, hundreds will be seen, mainly ranging from Waterford, along the west coast and up to the north coast of Donegal. During May and June, the cliffs of the Inishowen Peninsula, Ireland's most northerly point, are a good place from which to spot them. One of the vernacular names is *ainmhide na seolta* (monster with the sails), because of the huge tail fin. It is also known as the 'sun-fish' because of its habit of basking near the surface on sunny days.[iii] *Cetorhinus maximus* is the largest fish in the north Atlantic, and the second largest in the world (after the whale shark). The usual length is five to seven metres, but the longest known individual was over twelve metres. It swims around with its massive mouth open, straining dozens of kilos of plankton per day into its digestive system. Seen from above, they are huge-headed, majestic creatures, swinging their rudder of a tail from side-to-side as they curve slowly through the water. Basking sharks migrate to deeper waters in the autumn, but occasionally they go farther. In 2012, a shark tagged off Donegal travelled over five thousand kilometres to tropical waters off West Africa. In 2019, another shark, also tagged off Donegal, was photographed off Cape Cod in Massachusetts.

31st Geese that have overwintered in Ireland are starting to make the journey north to their various breeding grounds. Pale-bellied brent geese from Dublin Bay have been stopping to feed at Carlingford Lough and at Killough in

County Down. They will eventually end up in eastern High Arctic Canada via Iceland and Greenland. Meanwhile, the huge population of Greenland white-fronted geese (around 8,500), which winters in the Wexford Slobs, is also on the move. They usually begin to depart around now and continue to do so over the coming weeks. Like all geese, they travel in groups composed of family units, and let warm winds from the south help them on their way. They also break the journey in Iceland, a destination they can reach in eighteen hours if assisted by a following wind. Barnacle geese from Greenland, which overwinter in the west of Ireland, likewise stop in Iceland. The arduous journey can burn a huge amount of fat: up to a third of a goose's body weight. It takes several weeks to build up their reserves again.

April

1st Ladybirds have been emerging over the last few weeks, crawling out of their hiding places in hollow plant stems, curled leaves, cracks under windowsills and other sheltered niches. The most frequently seen species is the seven-spot ladybird. Individuals appear on warm walls and in clusters on plants, moving dozily, as if they have not yet shaken off their winter slumbers. After their lengthy hibernation they must feed up before they can mate, and – in the case of females – lay eggs. The principal food of the seven-spot, in common with most Irish ladybirds, is aphids. If aphids are scarce, as sometimes happens in early spring, it will eat other foods, including pollen and nectar. However, without adequate aphids, egg production will be reduced or prevented. The harlequin ladybird, an alien which became established in Ireland about a dozen years ago (with the first breeding population reported in Cork), competes with the natives for food; it also readily eats other ladybirds. The harlequin is faster to identify and consume prey, which is one of the reasons it was used as a biological control for pests in some countries.

2nd Easter week often falls in this month, so let us consider some of the flora and fauna associated with it. On the first Good Friday, according to folklore collected in various counties, Christ's crown of thorns was made from blackthorn, blackberry or rose briars. The violet droops, it was said, because the shadow of the cross fell on it. Various stories have an ever-changing cast of birds present at the crucifixion, but the robin is always there, getting splashed with blood and forever staining its breast red. A Tipperary tale tells of the robin taking the nails away from the cross, while the magpie kept bringing them back. The magpie is therefore a cursed bird. Stories collected in Ballycorus, south County Dublin, tell of the lapwing (*philibin*) flying over the cross and screeching 'Crucify him! Crucify him', while the heron's cry was 'Give him strength to endure his pain.' After that, it was said, he was not molested by his enemies. (And, when you think about it, few animals will mess with a heron.)

3rd Outside the breeding season it can be difficult to tell the difference between a shag and a cormorant unless you have a pair of binoculars. The cormorant is somewhat larger, but both are sizeable, black, prehistoric-looking diving birds that perch on coastal rocks. Both fly horizontally over the water in a straight and purposeful line. The cormorant can sometimes be identified when flying by its slightly kinked neck. It also frequents inland lakes, whereas shags are sea birds. At present, though, the shag is unmistakable, for it is sporting a splendid, forward-curling quiff. Both sexes are similarly ornamented during the breeding season. Research has suggested that birds with larger crests are more successful breeders. Cormorants and shags are monogamous, and often form pair bonds lasting from year to year. Both parents take turns incubating the eggs by holding them between their feet and breasts. They also share feeding duties.

4th The first spring gentians are blooming in the Burren. They will continue to flower for several weeks, peaking in May. *Gentiana verna* is the signature plant of the area: its upstanding, art nouveau flowers offer up petals of the purest blue. Their colour inspired the nineteenth-century American poet William Cullen Bryant to write: 'Blue – blue – as if the sky let fall a flower from its own caerulean wall.' The gentian, which arrived after the last ice age, is an Arctic-alpine species.

Its more usual habitat is on the higher slopes of the Pyrenees and the Alps. The high light levels in the Burren – with sunlight reflected both by the limestone and the sea – and the lack of competition from larger plants allow the gentian to thrive. Carefully managed winter grazing by cattle, known as 'winterage', keeps grasses and other plants in check. The spring gentian also grows on the Aran Islands and from the Burren up to southeast Mayo.

5th Five tern species come to Ireland to breed during the warmer months: Sandwich, Arctic, little, common and roseate terns. All have forked tails, short legs and black beanies. Their split tails and lively flight give them the colloquial name of 'sea swallows'. The Sandwich terns are the largest, about the size of a small gull. They are the first to return and have been trickling in from Africa since March. These and other terns can be seen in coastal waters dive-bombing for small fish. They are vocal birds, screeching and crying as they perform their aerobatics. Soon they will move to their communal breeding places. The tiny islands of Rockabill off north County Dublin are a globally important sanctuary for the roseate tern, with the largest breeding colony in Europe, which extends as far as the

Azores, home to another large colony. Each year about fifteen hundred pairs (nearly 50 per cent of the European population) nest here, as well as two thousand pairs of common terns, and hundreds of Arctic terns. Lady's Island Lake, near Rosslare, in County Wexford is another valuable breeding place. Its terrain – low, flat and grassy – is completely different from steep and rocky Rockabill, but both have rich fishing grounds nearby. In both locations, more aggressive birds such as common terns and black-headed gulls keep predators away. Roseate terns usually nest in crevices, but wooden nest boxes have been supplied for many years, and the birds have happily adapted.

6th Sometimes, while walking along the edge of a birch or ash wood, you may notice that the trunks are covered in dark, brownish spots. Some are hand-sized; some are larger. These irregular polka dots, which give a cartoonish look to the trees, are a leafy liverwort of the *Frullania* genus, possibly dilated scalewort (*F. dilatata*). Use a hand lens to get a closer look, or take a picture with your phone and zoom in. You will see that the splotches have tiny, flattened leaves: these are easiest to detect on the edges, where they spread out like mossy embroidery. A more familiar example of this group of plants is the common liverwort (*Marchantia polymorpha*). A subspecies often grows abundantly on the surface of compost in flowerpots, especially in plant nurseries. Its soft, fleshy lobes are typical examples of how this plant got the 'liver' part of its name. In the doctrine of signatures, concoctions of the plant were used for liver complaints.[iv]

7th Skylarks are singing. The song is an uninterrupted stream of whistling, warbling notes uttered from on high, fifty to a hundred metres in the air. It is high-pitched and far-carrying, populating the whole sky with its light sweetness. After each bout of singing – which can last up to half an hour – the bird floats down to earth and merges into the vegetation. The skylark's habitat is in open areas such as rough pasture and heathland, where it nests on the ground. The species' range has contracted, and the population has declined by over 30 per cent: intensification of farming has not helped. Eggs hatch after just twelve days, the shortest incubation period of any Irish bird. Chicks develop strong legs, and can scurry before they can fly. Within a week they scatter from the nest, hiding separately among tussocks and subshrubs. The parents continue to feed them until they are able to take to the air and become fully independent, after about three weeks.

8th Fumitory is in bloom. This little weed of waysides and waste ground bears upright stems with flowers that, when in bud, look like pink grains of rice tipped with wine. When they open, the ends gape, beak-like, just far enough to allow bees to insert their tongues to get at the nectar. The leaves are grey-green and diaphanous. If you are fanciful, a mass of it might look like smoke coming from the ground. Indeed, the mediaeval name was *fumus terrae* – smoke of the earth. It was believed that the plant arose spontaneously: 'engendered of a coarse fumosity rising from the earth' in the words of the sixteenth-century *Grete Herball*, the first herbal written in English, a compendium of information taken from earlier works. Fumitory is a member of the poppy family, although the flowers are decidedly un-poppyish. Gardeners, however, will see the foliage's similarity to that of the California poppy. Other wild poppies – corn poppy, opium poppy and the horned poppy of the seaside – will not bloom for several weeks.

9th Buzzards are present in every county. They are visible in the sky, gliding on air currents with their great wings (up to 1.3 metres) stiffly spread. As pairs enter the breeding season in the coming weeks, the flight of the male becomes more acrobatic. He executes rolling and spiralling dives, demonstrating his energy and fitness to his mate. Persecution by humans rendered buzzards extinct in Ireland at the end of the nineteenth century. However, birds returned from Scotland a few decades later and were recorded breeding at Rathlin Island in County Antrim in 1933. This population died out, possibly because myxomatosis drastically reduced the rabbit population, one of their principal foods. The late 1960s saw another movement from Scotland, and later on, an influx from Wales. In recent years, the population has increased dramatically, although colonisation is slow in the west. Illegal poisoning continues in some areas. Buzzards feed on small prey and carrion, and help keep balance in nature. They are apex predators, helping to control medium predators such as magpies and other members of the crow family.

10th Keep an eye on roadside banks and wasteland, and you may see the pale nose-cones of tiny rockets pushing up from the ground. These are the first shoots of field horsetail (*Equisetum arvense*), a primitive plant that has its ancestors in the Carboniferous Period, over 300 million years ago. Those prehistoric horsetails, known as calamites, were the size of trees. Their descendants are miniatures in comparison. The tallest Irish species – great horsetail, an inhabitant of moist clay soil – reaches two metres. Horsetails reproduce by spores instead of seeds: the ivory-coloured shoots appearing now are the fertile stems. They lack chlorophyll, and instead bear cream, cone-like strobili, which release the spores. The normal shoots, which usually appear weeks later, are green and conspicuously jointed. They can be pulled apart at the nodes and temporarily stuck back together again, prompting the vernacular name, 'Lego plant'. All horsetails contain silica in their stems, which makes them abrasive. They were traditionally used for scouring pots and metalwork.

11th Ireland's estuaries are emptying of their winter visitors, including wading birds from colder regions such as Greenland, Iceland, Siberia and the Scandinavian peninsula. Their winter stays are considerably longer than their summer trips 'home' to breed. The first usually arrive here in July and August and they stay until at least March and often into May. The long bills of waders are adapted to probe the estuarine mud in search of prey: shellfish, crustaceans, worms and other invertebrates. For many of us, these birds are a confusing jumble: a mixum-gatherum of avian balls-on-sticks. One species, however, is beginning to stand out from the rest. Black-tailed godwits are putting on their startling breeding plumage and are easily identified. Their long-legged elegance is breathtaking: head, breast and neck are suffused with a sumptuous orange-brown that leaches into the black and pale mosaic of their hindquarters. Our wintering population comes from Iceland, and is a distinct race, with rich colouring.

12th On beaches, sea beet is punctuating the shingle with its huddles of shiny, triangular leaves. As the season progresses it will sprawl farther and send out thin, knobbly flower spikes. The flowers of *Beta vulgaris* subsp. *maritima* are wind-pollinated and offer no nectar rewards to flying insects. The plant's value to wildlife is not immediately obvious, but the tightly packed leaves offer shelter for ground-dwelling invertebrates. They are also the larval food of the sea groundling, a leaf-mining moth. The plant is the wild ancestor of some of our crops, including sugar beet, spinach beet, beetroot and chard. The seedlings, crowded around the parent plants now, have white-and-pink stems and green cotyledons (first leaves) held upwards like praying hands.

They will look familiar to gardeners who grow their relatives. Sea beet is tastiest before the flowers form, but if foraging, avoid dog-walking areas as the plants are often marked as enthusiastically as lamp posts.

13th There is an abundance of curlews here during winter. Throughout the chilly months, wetlands and mudflats are thronged with the brown birds, our largest waders. They probe sand, mud, rock pools and clumps of seaweed with their fabulously long and curved bills, winkling out worms, shellfish and crustaceans. Yet, most are migrants from Scandinavia, Scotland and other northerly regions. Our own breeding population may number no more than 150 pairs, a catastrophic loss from the thousands that bred here just forty years ago. Curlews are in danger of extinction in Ireland. Our resident curlews have moved inland now and are nesting on the ground in boglands, wet grassland and rough pastures. About four eggs are laid, hatching after four weeks. But breeding success is rare, thanks to habitat destruction and predation by fox, mink, hooded crow and magpie. If you see pairs nesting, do keep your distance, and report the sighting to BirdWatch Ireland.

14th Buttercups are appearing in pastures and on road verges. Their scientific name, *Ranunculus*, comes from the Latin for frog, *rana*, because so many of the family grow in damp places. One section of the clan that illustrates this preference perfectly is the crowfoot sub-genus, all of which grow either in wet mud or water. The flowers are distinctly buttercuppish, but with white petals. All have golden bosses of stamens at the centre. The name crowfoot was once given to others in the family, including buttercups and wood anemone, because of the shape of the leaves. However, the appellation stuck only with this watery branch of the tribe, even though it poorly describes their foliage, which may be round-lobed, ivy-like or thread-leaved, depending on the species. Water crowfoots in streams and rivers can change the dynamics of flow and thus increase biodiversity. Colonies of the plants slow the speed of the water, which allows sediments to lie and other vegetation such as watercress to develop. This creates a congenial habitat for invertebrates, including caddisfly, mayfly and dragonfly larvae. These creatures, in turn, can provide nutrition for fish and water birds. Increased flow beyond the crowfoot keeps the riverbed free from silt.

15th The natterjack toad is calling at night in a ratchet-y voice like a clockwork key being wound in a hollow toy. Ireland's rarest amphibian probably numbers fewer than ten thousand adults. It is confined to a few coastal regions in County Kerry and – following a successful introduction in the 1990s – the Raven Nature Reserve in County Wexford. The toad is widely distributed across Europe, ranging in a diagonal swathe from Portugal up to the Baltic coast. There are a few isolated populations in Britain. How did it end up in Ireland? It may have arrived after the last Ice Age, along with the mysterious Lusitanian flora (which includes Saint Patrick's cabbage and the large-flowered Saint Dabeoc's heath) found only in southwest Ireland and a few other places, including the Iberian Peninsula. But the first record was relatively late: it was seen in 1805 by James Townsend Mackay, the author of *Flora Hibernica*. A local story tells that quantities of toads were once released from a ship at the head of Dingle Bay. Implausible perhaps, except that ships commonly dumped sand they had carried as ballast, and the toads live among sand dunes (as well as coastal marsh and heathland). Whatever its provenance, the natterjack is red-listed as endangered. Since 2008, over a hundred artificial ponds have been created in County Kerry, and the toad has started to colonise them.

16th Among the leafy ingredients in the bags of mixed salad in the supermarket is lamb's lettuce, also known as corn salad. The rosettes of small, spatulate leaves often have trailing roots attached. Look down next time you are walking along a weedy footpath, and you may see similar plants poking out among the tufts of short meadow grass – another common pavement species. *Valerianella locusta*, the salad bag plant, is one of several lamb's lettuces that grow wild in Ireland. All are similar, and are identified only by their miniature seed pods: you need a microscope, scalpel and steady hand to tell the difference. Superficially the flowers resemble minuscule, mauve forget-me-nots, but they are not related. They belong to the honeysuckle family (*Caprifoliaceae*), a clan that also includes the lofty, spiny teasel and the red valerian of walls. The leaves are young and tasty during lambing season, which accounts for the 'lamb' in the name. 'Corn salad' designates it as a weed of grain fields.

17th Vine weevils are starting to appear in unexpected places indoors: slowly trundling up stairs or meandering across tables. They may have come from houseplants or have hitched a ride on your clothing when you were in the garden. Originally native to continental Europe, *Otiorhynchus* *sulcatus* has spread all over the world via the nursery trade. The pea-sized weevil is a dull, black-and-brown insect with a domed, corrugated back and an elongated snout. Look at it under a hand lens and you'll see that it is a handsome creature, well-formed in all its parts and with irregular tufts of golden hairs on its back. Underground and in pots, the creamy larvae are consuming plant roots. They are about to pupate, a stage when they look as if they are coated in white chocolate. They will emerge in early summer as adults, feeding at night-time on foliage and leaving jagged incisions around the margins of leaves. Those that are rambling about now are probably last year's generation: they live for two or more years. Vine weevils belong to a group of insects that can reproduce without fertilisation (a process known as parthenogenesis). In this species, all the resulting offspring are female. Males have never been documented. Newly emerged individuals are able to lay eggs within about four weeks.

18th Cowslips used to be so abundant that they were picked by the hundreds and used as remedies for many afflictions, including jaundice, measles, chickenpox, pleurisy, insomnia and sore fingers. In Kilkenny, according to records in the National Folklore Collection, 'an ointment made with hog's lard and the flowers of the cowslip removes wrinkles and spots from the skin of the face and restores youth'. The plant was supposed to cure palsy, leading to the vernacular name of palsywort. The flowers were also collected and made into 'toss balls': playthings for children created by tightly stringing dozens of flower heads together. *Primula veris* almost disappeared, thanks to intensive agriculture and the overuse of herbicides on verges. But it is making a comeback now: look for it on old pastures and along roadsides. Occasionally it crosses with the primrose to make the false oxlip, which has multiple primrose-like flower heads on single stems.

19th Passengers in cars on motorways are often treated to views of raptors soaring overhead searching for prey. The long grass on verges shelters small mammals, while the tarmac and hard shoulders may be the resting place for roadkill. Kestrels, which hunt rodents such as mice and shrews, hover in one place with wings a-flutter, scanning for their next meal. They are about the same size as a sparrowhawk but have more slender wings. The red kite, a recent reintroduction to Ireland, has a wingspan of up to 1.8 metres, over twice that of the kestrel or sparrowhawk. The rusty tones of its body and inner wings are obvious in good light. The forked tail is an identifier. Birds were introduced to counties Wicklow and Dublin, and have since bred also in Meath and Wexford, so these regions offer the best opportunities for sighting. The red kite takes small mammals and birds, and – in leaner times – carrion. The buzzard, which we encountered earlier this month, is another motorway bird of prey. It has recolonised Ireland naturally over the last fifty years. With broader wings than those of the red kite, it looks chunkier and browner.

20th As spring brings humans out into the garden, our tidying and general busy-ness spell disruption for the millions of invertebrates sharing our properties. Paradoxically, one of the easiest of these small creatures to identify is one that allows us the most fleeting of glances. Lift up a pot, or fork through the compost heap, and the common brown centipede (*Lithobius forficatus*) is just a skitter of scurrying, rust-coloured legs and undulating body – and then it's gone. The stone centipede, as it is also known, is a predator of other invertebrates, as well as a consumer of decaying matter. It is most active at night. Occasionally it wanders into houses and sheds. The old joke: 'What goes ninety-nine, thump, ninety-nine, thump? A centipede with a wooden leg' is quite inaccurate for this species. *L. forficatus* has seven pairs of legs when newly hatched, and fifteen when mature, a total of thirty individual legs. Twenty-nine, thump, twenty-nine, thump.

21st Garden birds are enthusiastically occupied with family life. A few are sitting on eggs. Thrushes, blackbirds and robins are among the earliest to breed, and may already be feeding families of hungry chicks. Their nestlings need to eat invertebrates to thrive, but the adult diet is more varied. Make sure there are high-fat seeds (such as sunflower hearts) and perhaps some mealworms on a bird table. Not all birds can balance on a hanging feeder. The above species usually raise at least two broods in a season. Collared doves, wood pigeons and feral pigeons also breed multiple times. The first two build flimsy platforms in trees, while the last often chooses quiet ledges on buildings. Other birds are hurriedly building nests and are looking for materials: small twigs, wisps of grass, moss, lichen, spider webs, feathers and hair. If you have a dog that you brush, leave bundles of hair for the birds, but not if the dog was treated for fleas.

22nd Cuckoo flower is in bloom, sprinkling damp roadsides, meadows and fields with its dainty, four-petalled, luminously lilac flowers. It is so named because it appears at the time when the cuckoo begins to call. *Cardamine pratensis* has a host of other common names, including lady's smock and milking maids. Their origins are complicated, but the associations were often bawdy. Christianity, however, with its habitual sanitising compulsions gave this plant (along with many others) to the Virgin Mary. The flowers range from pinky-purple to nearly white, which explains Shakespeare's 'lady-smocks all silver-white ... Do paint the meadows with delight.' It is the food plant of two butterfly caterpillars, the orange-tip and the green-veined

white. The meadow longhorn moth also lays her eggs on it.
She is a tiny, elegant creature with greenish, bronzed wings
and greatly elongated, curving antennae. Froghopper nymphs
may inhabit its stems and stalks, safely protected in balls of
frothy spit.

23rd Duckling season is upon us. The first tiny mallard
chicks are on the water, zipping about after their
mothers like fluffy, clockwork bumblebees. The colours of
their downy plumage are a mixture of pale straw and dark
brown, while a strong dark stripe runs through the yellow
face, across the eye. The female lays nine to thirteen eggs. In
areas where there is a high density of breeding birds, other
mallards (and even other duck species) will sometimes 'egg
dump' into nests. This ensures the continuation of their genes
without the bother of having to rear a brood. Male mallards
do not look after their young, and may even attack and kill
unaccompanied ducklings. The risk to young mallards is
greatest in the first two weeks of their lives, and they may
be killed by gulls, herons, magpies, rats, mink and other
predators. Large clutch sizes make up for the fairly high rate
of attrition.

24th Street trees are changing day by day, filling out
with leaves and putting out flowers. Cherries of
several varieties are in bloom and are covered in white or
pink blossom. Mostly the flowers are 'double', meaning that
they have many extra petals. Often this is at the expense of
the reproductive organs, so most will produce no fruits, or
very few. Members of the maple family are bearing clusters
of flowers, and are unfolding their first angular leaves. Some
estates and suburban roads have plantings of Japanese maples,
while our urban streets are fringed with larger members of
the same family: Norway maple, sycamore and London plane.
Lime trees, which line some of our grander roads, will bloom

in the coming weeks, producing bunches of sweetly scented flowers that are much visited by pollinators. Fastigiate hornbeams, shaped like teardrops, punctuate median strips and verges on some larger roads. They are fully clothed in leaves now.

25th Today is Saint Mark's Day, a day that has its very own insect. Saint Mark's flies seemingly arrive from nowhere around this time, appearing on woodland edges and along hedgerows. These jet-black flies hang about for a couple of weeks, often in sizeable swarms, and then disappear. *Bibio marci* is an elongated fly with a shiny abdomen that gleams through its coat of abundant hairs. Its tremendously long legs dangle while it drifts jerkily through the air. Also known as the hawthorn fly, its hatch often coincides with the flowering of that plant. It is a harmless insect, doing no damage to humans, livestock or crops. It feeds on flowers and acts as a pollinator. The larvae live on decaying matter and the roots of grass. Adults that stray over streams or lakes are eagerly snatched by fish. Anglers going after trout sometimes use a faux fly modelled on this insect.

26th House martins are returning from Africa in increasing numbers. Unlike swallows, they have completely white undercarriages; and their tails, while forked, are a little shorter. In flight, their rumps gleam whitely, unlike those of swallows, which are dark. True to their name, house martins often choose the outside of a house for their nests, which they tuck under the eaves or fascia boards – a habitat that mimics overhanging rock ledges. Try to get a look at their extraordinary legs while they are building a nest or collecting mud. The limbs are covered with feathers, the only passerine bird that is thus outfitted. The purpose of these feathery trousers is not certain, but they may provide the answer to one of ornithology's mysteries. It is not clear where house martins go when they leave their summer quarters. Small numbers are seen in tropical Africa, but nothing that equates to an overwintering population. These insulating feathers have led ornithologists to speculate that the birds spend the non-breeding period on the wing. Toasty warm in their head-to-toe feathers, they may be riding on air currents in the chilly clouds above African rain forests.

27th Bluebells are in flower, forming shimmering mists of blue in woodlands and other shady places. Sometimes the flowers pop up among bracken: these may be the survivors of scrubland or woods that have been cleared. Our native bluebell (*Hyacinthoides non-scripta*) has flowers on one side of a gracefully arching stalk. The Spanish bluebell (*H. hispanica*) is paler and sturdier, with flowers all around the stalk. It is a garden escape; the earliest record of its becoming naturalised is from 1887, in Howth. The two species cross readily and produce fertile hybrids, giving rise to a range of mongrel bluebells. In Irish folk medicine, the chopped roots of *coinnle corra* were used to draw out boils. When cooked with other plants and mixed with goat's butter, the roots were also a remedy for rickets. Bluebells are a source of early nectar and are visited by bees, hoverflies and butterflies. They are the food plant for the larvae of the autumnal rustic and the six-striped rustic moths. Bluebell woods to visit include Clogrennane Wood, County Carlow; Lough Key Forest Park, County Roscommon; Killinthomas Wood and Moore Abbey Wood, County Kildare; and Belleek Woods and Raheens Wood in County Mayo.

28th Southeast winds in springtime sometimes bring unexpected birds. One such curiosity is the hoopoe. Approximately the size of a thrush, it looks as if a comic-book artist has drawn it. Head and body are faded rusty orange, while the wings are precisely striped in black and white. An extravagant head crest fans forward and back depending on the hoopoe's level of excitement. The dark bill is a long, precise set of tweezers, perfect for plucking larvae and other invertebrates out of grass and tree bark. Most years a few individuals are seen in southern counties, where they land in open areas of short grass, often at the sides of roads or in fields. In 2015, over fifty birds were reported, and unusually, some were seen as far north as Mayo, Louth and Donegal. Hoopoes that stray to Ireland are members of a southern European population that have overshot their home place while travelling back from wintering in Africa. The common name is often pronounced 'hoo-poo'. Both it and the scientific name (a mix of Latin and Greek: *Upupa epops*) reflect the bird's eerie and beautiful 'hoo-hoo … hoo-hoo-hoo' song.

29th The Kerry slug is a protected and mysterious species, occurring only in the southwest of Ireland and the northwest of Spain and Portugal. Dublin naturalist William Andrews first found *Geomalacus maculosus* in 1842 by Caragh Lake, near Castlemaine in County Kerry. According to a paper published by the Royal Dublin Society some years later, Andrews 'placed it in the hands of Dr. Allman [George James Allman, ecologist, botanist and zoologist]; and it was first exhibited at a meeting of the Dublin Natural History Society in January 1843'. It is a large slug, with two distinct colour morphs, each matching the terrain where it is found. In woodlands, it is brown with yellow spots, merging into the tones of damp tree bark and moss. In more open situations, such as blanket bogs, it is black with white spots, easily disappearing into a landscape punctuated with lichen-encrusted rocks. Research published in 2011 found that the greatest numbers in a woodland habitat were found in April, May and June, while October, November and December saw peak numbers in a blanket bog. The slug's normal diet consists of lichens, mosses, liverworts and fungi. However, nineteenth-century mollusc specialist D. F. Heynemann kept Irish slugs in captivity for a winter, feeding them foods that included lettuce and – according to a contemporary writer – gherkins. The Kerry slug is nocturnal, but it also comes out on dull, wet days throughout the year. Two of its strongholds are the Glengarriff Nature Reserve in west Cork and Uragh Wood in County Kerry.

30th Marsh marigold is in flower. It grows on the soggy edges of waterways, in ditches and on soil that is waterlogged in winter. It coats the ground with heart-shaped leaves and clusters of rich yellow flowers and is bold and splashy in a way that is incongruous for a wildflower. This magnificence is reflected in one of the common names, kingcup. Its membership of the buttercup family is obvious by the colour and formation of the flowers. *Caltha palustris* is also known as May-flower, as well as *lus buí Bealtaine* (the yellow Bealtaine plant). In times past it was gathered today, on May eve, along with primroses, cowslips and buttercups. These yellow flowers were tied into bunches and hung over doors and windows. Sometimes they were simply strewn on doorsteps and other entrances, including those to farm buildings. They were believed to protect the inhabitants and their animals from evil. In Wexford, garlands were put on cattle and hung on door-posts to ward off 'the fairy power'.

May

1st Hawthorn, the may bush, is in flower, although after harsh springs it can be late. Also known as whitethorn – and *sceach gheal* in Irish – it puts on its foliage before its flowers, unlike its relatives blackthorn and cherry plum, which bloom on bare stems. The lobed leaves are unmistakable, and they form a green backdrop for the effervescent white blossom. The blooming is at its most dramatic in the Burren, where the pale grey limestone walls are bordered by gnarled trees, their tops sculpted and shorn by the wind. Hawthorn has been used as a livestock-proof hedging plant for centuries, and is then known as quicks or quicksett. Lone hawthorn trees are often seen in farm fields, with crops growing all around them. Although their presence must slow down the machinery, local history establishes them as 'fairy trees' and cutting them down is deemed unlucky.

2nd Whimbrels are visiting us now, stopping in coastal areas on their journey north, after wintering in southern Spain and along the west African coast. They pause here for refuelling on their way home to breed in northern Europe – mostly Iceland. A few may mate and nest closer to us, in the Hebrides or Shetland Islands. The whimbrel is related to the curlew, but is smaller, with pretty dark stripes along the crown and through the eye. Some of its vernacular names reflect the relationship: half curlew, May curlew and May whaap (Ulster Scots for curlew). It is also known simply as the May bird. Often you will hear whimbrels overhead before you see them, a swift staccato call, as if played on a piccolo: 'pip-pip-pip-pip-pip-pip-pip'. They fly in small groups and land to probe estuary mud and seaweed for crustaceans, shellfish and marine worms.

3rd Many spring flowers are yellow, regardless of their structure or family. Think of all the sunny-bloomed wild plants around now: coltsfoot, dandelion, lesser celandine, cowslip, primrose, marsh marigold, black medick, hedge mustard, wood avens, buttercup, broom and gorse. In the vegetable garden, last year's brassicas are a-flutter with delicate yellow petals. Daffodils still dance on roadsides. The purpose of all this canary-coloured florescence is unclear, but there are several theories. Flower pigment acts as a signal to pollinators, and with fewer insects around in spring, yellow may be a strong attractant, more visible from a distance than other colours. Yellow also reflects light and heat onto the plant's reproductive organs, perhaps causing them to be more efficient. It may also make the flower a warmer and more comfortable place for the insect to land and gather pollen and nectar. Whatever the reason, all that yellow is certainly cheering.

4th Uninterrupted early morning sleeps can be difficult this month, as the birds launch into a full-throated dawn chorus. For most of us, it is the complicated, many-phrased and melodic song of the blackbird that acts as an alarm clock. His voice is soon joined by those of the robin, song thrush and wren. These early birds are the species with the largest eyes: they are able to gather more light and are thus able to see better in the dimness. As brightness seeps across the sky, wood pigeons, hooded crows, rooks, warblers, finches, sparrows and other birds join in. Great tits and blue tits sing in the morning, but are more voluble at night. In rural areas with open grassland or bog, the skylark is one of the earliest birds to rise, often singing just after four a.m. at this time of the year. If you fancy getting up with the lark, local branches of Birdwatch Ireland run dawn chorus events throughout the country in May.

5th Goosegrass, cleavers, sticky-backs, sticky willy or even *Galium aparine*: whatever you call it, this annual plant of roadsides and gardens is a delight for children and a scourge for gardeners. The square-stemmed plant, with its whorls of leaves poking out like wheel spokes along its length, is covered from top to tail in hooked bristles. These make it adhere magically to clothes and hair, but also allow it to hoist itself through and over other plants as it grows. The white, almost invisible, starry flowers produce tiny green burrs, like furry ball-bearings. These stick to passing animals, including humans, ensuring that the next generation of robin-run-the-hedge (as it is also known) is dispersed far and wide. Goosegrass, as the name suggests, was fed to geese (and hens). It is a member of the bedstraw family, a clan that includes the scented lady's bedstraw and sweet woodruff.

6th Swifts are arriving in force from central and southern Africa. They fly about eight hundred kilometres per day, across jungles, the Sahara, the Atlas Mountains, the Mediterranean and Spain. They feed as they fly, opening the beak into a tremendously wide gape, the better to efficiently capture insects. The first often appear around mid-April, but there is usually only a trickle of birds until the first week of May. Swifts stay with us for just three months, but this is their breeding place. Birds mate with the same partner year after year, if both have survived. They arrive back in Ireland separately, but they return to the same nesting place where they meet again. Mated pairs raise one or two chicks, and parents and offspring return to Africa within six to eight weeks of hatching. The young will not mate until their second or third year, and will spend the intervening time in the air. They eat, drink and sleep on the wing.

7th Wild arum is poking up its curious, cowled inflorescences at the base of hedgerows and along woodland edges. The spadix-and-spathe arrangement looks like a purple or greenish-yellow baseball bat nestling inside a pale green hood. *Arum maculatum* has so many common names that they would spill out of this small space. The late writer and naturalist Geoffrey Grigson recorded ninety. Among them are lords and ladies, Adam and Eve, bulls and cows and cuckoo pint – all of which pay tribute to the phallic spadix embraced by the female-seeming spathe. In Irish it is *cluas chaoin* or *cluas an ghabhair*, meaning narrow ear or goat's ear. Tiny flies are attracted by the faintly rank odour and become trapped in the chamber below the spadix, where the minute flowers are hidden out of sight. After unwittingly pollinating the plant, they find their way out, only to tumble into another arum abyss.

8th Pipistrelle bats have been on the wing for the last couple of weeks, zigzagging rapidly through the air as they hawk for flies and midges. They appear soon after sundown, when flying insects are abundant. During the day they roost in tree crevices and in niches in buildings, including under fascia boards and tiles. They spent the winter and early spring in hibernation – where exactly is not known, as there are few records of hibernating pipistrelles. We have nine species of bat, but the most frequently seen are the common and soprano pipistrelles – the bats of urban areas. Both are tiny, weighing just a few grams each. The soprano is slightly smaller and has a higher-pitched squeak, but the two are impossible to differentiate without special equipment. Bat calls are beyond our range of hearing, so a bat detector that measures ultrasound frequencies must be used.

9th Spring squill is in bloom in a few coastal locations on the eastern and northern edges of Ireland. It favours the short grass along cliff paths and coastal walks, and it is largely immune to salt spray. The tiny bulb usually grows in colonies that can be spotted from ten metres or more away – as if someone has sprinkled the ground with blue confetti. The sight of them demands that you scramble or crawl to get a closer look. The flowers, which sit among the curling bootlace leaves, are just a few centimetres tall, and are a clean blue, sometimes with a touch of mauve. The stamens are tipped with purple. They are not unlike flattened bluebells on stumpy stalks. *Scilla verna* is the county flower of County Down: an area where a large concentration of them has been recorded. In the Republic, County Wexford and north County Dublin offer the highest numbers.

10th Barnacles may look like miniature limpets, with their conical volcano-like shells, but the two are completely unrelated. Limpets are molluscs (as are mussels, periwinkles and oysters), while barnacles are crustaceans, a group that includes lobsters, crabs, shrimp and woodlice. These last all have 'legs', or some kind of jointed appendages – not something that is obvious in a barnacle. The legs are there, but they are neatly battened away when we most commonly see barnacles – at low tide. When the tide comes in, and the barnacle is underwater, the 'door' at the top opens. The feathery legs (known as cirri) sweep out and pull plankton and other organic matter into the shell. Plankton levels are high in spring, so barnacles are particularly busy feeding now. Much of our understanding of these creatures is thanks to Charles Darwin, who wrote two volumes, *Living Cirripedia*, just before publishing *The Origin of Species*.

11th The Burren is in bloom. Probably the most widespread and noticeable species is mountain avens (*Dryas octopetala*), a diminutive member of the rose family. It has low-growing, yellow-bossed, creamy flowers and tiny, shiny oak-like leaves – dark green above and whitish underneath. It grows mainly in limestone heath, where it squeezes into niches next to the pale grey rocks, pressing its mats of leathery foliage against their heat-retaining surface. It is an 'Arctic-alpine' species, more at home in Arctic and subarctic regions and above 2,500 metres in the Alps. Spring gentian (*Gentiana verna*), another Burren special, with purest blue petals unfolding from a prettily whorled bud, is a plant of alpine meadows. It is finished blooming in many locations, but in some areas flowers still persist. A few bloody cranesbill (*Geranium sanguineum*) may be peeping out precociously, but the main flush of this shocking-pink-flowered miniature is yet to come. The first of the many orchids, the early purple orchid, is marching across tracts of limestone scrub and pasture with its deep violet batons of bloom.

12th The chaffinch's call is almost a monotonous repetition of its name: 'chaff-finch … chaff-finch-finch'. But its song is sweet: a short run of trills that descends into a warble. The female is a drab olive-brown and is sometimes confused with the sparrow – but the chalky white wing bars are an identifier. The male, especially now in the breeding season, is a handsome fellow with a pinky-russet vest, a blue-grey cap, a brownish back and dark, white-barred wings. Both sexes have slightly back-swept head feathers, giving them a perky look. Females are sitting on eggs now: a single brood of four or five chicks will hatch. In wintertime our population is swelled by chaffinches from northern Europe. Females often migrate farther than males, so when the Swedish scientist, Linnaeus, observed all-male flocks in winter, he named them *Fringilla coelebs* – the bachelor finch.

13th Hedgerows, woodland edges and roadsides are spangled with the pure white flowers of greater stitchwort. It is a leaner and a scrambler, with brittle stems that rely on other plants for support. Each of the five petals on the blooms of *Stellaria holostea* is deeply divided, adding to the glittering, starry look. Those of lesser stitchwort (*S. graminea*), are even more distinctly lobed, so that each flower looks as if it has ten petals. In vernacular medicine, chewing stitchwort was supposed to cure stitches in the side and other pains. Among its common names are devil's corn and devil's skirt buttons – thus called not for any satanic qualities, but more in the jocular vein of 'little devil'. Chickweed (*S. media*), the straggling annual plant of vegetable gardens and waste ground, belongs to the same genus. Examine the tiny flowers, and you'll see that they are of a similar format.

14th Kittiwakes spend half the year out at sea, but in recent weeks they have come in to the coast to form huge colonies on cliffs. Near Dublin, there are hundreds-strong, rowdy gatherings on the sheer rock-faces at Howth and Bray Head. They nest on headlands all over Ireland, with the largest assembly (up to seven thousand birds) at the Cliffs of Moher in County Clare. The species is monogamous each season, often pairing with the same bird from the previous year. The first few weeks back in the colony are spent in mate-seeking and bonding – pairs sit breast to breast and delicately nod and nudge. The kittiwake has a large head and plump body, making it a gentle-looking gull, an appearance at odds with its mewling, nasal and insistent call: 'kitti-WAKE … kitti-WAKE … kitti-WAKE'. The first eggs will be laid at the end of this month, in a messy nest of seaweed, grass and mud stuck onto a ledge. Kittiwake numbers have plummeted in recent years. This is partly due to a lack of small fish such as sandeels, which have been affected by rising sea temperatures and industrial fishing operations.

15th Our two white-flowered wild garlics are in bloom: the alien but naturalised three-cornered leek (*Allium triquetrum*) and the native ramsons (*A. ursinum*). The first is a gangly plant, superficially like a white bluebell, but with over-lush, angular stems and leaves that are prone to collapse. The indigenous species is shorter and prettier, with broad, paddle-shaped leaves and starry, six-petalled flowers borne in clusters in a loose umbrella. It populates hedgerows and woodlands, often covering shady ground with a thousands-strong, light-emitting, snowy carpet. Wild garlic has long been used as a spring tonic and as a cure for disorders of the blood and the respiratory system. The specific epithet, *ursinum*, is from the Latin for bear, as the plant – a native of northern Asia as well as Europe – was supposedly the first food that bears would eat in spring after waking up from hibernation.

16th Parks and gardens are brightened by the fluttering presences of butterflies: small tortoiseshells, holly blues, peacocks and all the whites. Among the last is the orange tip, a pretty butterfly that looks as if its forewings have been dipped in orange squash. That's the male: the female has no orange toning and could be mistaken for a small white. However, if you get a look at the undersides of her hindwings when she is 'nectaring', you'll see greenish markings, like splashes of algae. No other white (aside from her male counterpart) has this marbling. Females keep a low profile, flitting from plant to plant, while the males patrol an area methodically and very visibly. Orange tips are 'univoltine', raising one brood per year. The eggs are laid on any of several plants belonging to the cabbage family, especially cuckoo flower and garlic mustard. The latter, also known as jack-by-the-hedge, has bright-green, serrated leaves and a crown of small, four-petalled white flowers. The foliage has a slight whiff of garlic: all parts of the plant are eaten by foragers.

17th The iconic plant of country roadsides at this time of the year is cow parsley, crowding verges with its delicate and frothy white flowers. Vernacular names in Ireland include dog parsley and hare's parsley. These, along with the bovine forename, refer to the plant's inferior taste compared to its culinary relative, parsley. Don't be tempted to experiment unless you are a hundred per cent sure you have the right species. The *Apiaceae* family includes some very poisonous plants, among them hemlock, cowbane and hemlock water dropwort; all bear white umbels of flower, and could easily be mistaken for cow parsley. Another common name for *Anthriscus sylvestris* is Queen Anne's lace; some sources say that this refers not to a monarch, but to Saint Anne, the mother of Mary and patron saint of lacemakers. It was also sometimes called lady's lace, in honour of Mary, and was used to decorate May altars.

18th In the past few weeks gardens have suddenly become full of hoverflies hanging in the air, their wings whirring so fast that they are invisible. Watch an individual, and you'll see that it can remain suspended as if by an unseen string for minutes on end. Or rather, 'he' can do so – for these stalled-on-the-wing insects are males monitoring their territories. Occasionally one will see off a rival: quickly zipping off and barging into the interloper before returning to his position. There are 180 species of hoverfly – syrphids – in Ireland. A good number are bee or wasp mimics, with furry or stripy bodies, but they bear no stings and rely on their powers of deception to deter predators. Others are brown or blackish, however, and not as easy to recognise. Adults feed mostly on nectar and pollen, but the larvae of many feed on aphids.

19th Ribwort plantain (*Plantago lanceolata*) goes mostly unnoticed on the edges of paths, on waste ground, and in grassland (including lawns). The long leaves, marked by faint pleats of parallel veins, are ground-hugging and easily missed. The flower head, a long-standing structure that appears first in March, is a dark-brown bullet on a tall and limber stalk. For a few weeks (around now), the flower becomes fertile, producing an incongruously lacy and ethereal ruff of creamy anthers that shimmer delicately in the slightest breeze. In times past, children used the flower stems in games of 'fighting cocks' or 'soldiers'. The stem is looped under the head like a noose, sharply tugged and the head fires off at one's opponent. Alternatively, you can just bop your opponent with a whippy stem. *Slánlus*, which means health plant in Irish, has many traditional uses, including to prevent worms in farm animals, to staunch bleeding and to soothe nettle stings.

20th This is the time when cockchafers are bashing about at night, bumping into outdoor lights and bright windows and buzzing along with a deep, sonorous tone. Back garden entomologists sometimes find them in moth traps also. This large, brown beetle (up to three centimetres) is a member of the scarab family. It crawls up from below the soil during this month – earning it the vernacular name of May bug. It is also known as the doodlebug (a nickname that was used for the German V-1 flying bomb because of its distinctive buzz). The cockchafer lives for just a few weeks as an adult: most of its three-to-four-year life cycle is spent underground as a fat, ivory-coloured grub, munching on roots. Newly emerged May bugs appear covered in white powder. They have improbable-looking antennae, which can spread out like fans, the better to sense pheromones and other stimulants: males have seven ribs per fan, while females have six. In times past, cockchafer numbers were much diminished by widespread use of pesticides, but the species is seeing a resurgence.

21st Herb Robert is in bloom along hedgerows and woodland edges and in crevices in walls. It is one of the first properly pink flowers of the year, and its rosy stars are a sign of the season moving along. It is easily identified, with five-petalled flowers and pretty, much-divided, almost fernlike foliage – often tinged with red. Leaves, stems and even flower buds are covered in tiny, slightly sticky hairs. Plants have a faint odour, which has given rise to one of its many vernacular names: stinking Robert. It grows happily in urban settings, opportunistically inserting itself into cracks in paving. Caleb Threlkeld in his flora of 1726 noted that it grew under the hedges between Kilmainham gallows and Chapelizod Bridge. *Geranium robertianum* belongs to the same genus as the hardy geraniums of gardens: the kinds planted under roses and in herbaceous borders (not the red 'geranium' of window sills and porches – properly known as *Pelargonium*). Hardy geraniums are commonly known as cranesbills, and owe this name to the pointed seed pods that follow the flowers.

22nd Most times you see a dipper it is gone before you know it: a barely seen dash of dark wings and rotund body speeding low along a rocky river's course. If you're lucky you may catch a flash of its white bib as it races on its way. In Irish it is *gobha uisce*, meaning water blacksmith – perhaps because of its white apron. Pairs are nesting now, in holes in banks or bridges, or in crevices behind waterfalls. About two-thirds the size of a blackbird, the dipper has thick, robust legs that support it in fast-flowing water. Uniquely among songbirds, it dives and swims underwater for its food, often using its wings to stabilise itself. It can stay submerged for half a minute as it hunts for insect larvae, crustaceans and tiny fish. When it perches on the water's edge, it bobs with a curious, syncopated down-up, down-up motion, as if it is listening to its own dance track.

23rd Green alkanet is in flower, producing small, five-petalled, white-centred bowls of the clearest blue. The flower's contrasting core has given the plant the vernacular names of 'pheasant's eye' and 'bird's eye'. *Pentaglottis sempervirens* will flower for months, getting more straggly and untidy as it ages. Leaves and stems are bristly and coarse, as are those of many of its relatives in the borage family. It was brought to this country some centuries ago as a garden ornamental, or perhaps as a dye plant: the word alkanet comes via a circuitous route from the Arabic *al-henna*. The roots are supposed to produce a reddish colourant. Alkanet has spread slowly since its introduction, and is most often found near buildings, ruins or roadsides, or on waste ground. Each flower produces only four heavy seeds, which fall straight to the ground – a lazy method of dispersal. Once it gains a foothold, though, it is very tenacious, boring downwards with a long tap root.

24th Look carefully at the flowers in a pesticide-free garden and you may be lucky enough to spot a crab spider waiting for her prey. The female *Misumena vatia* is yellow-green or pearly white, sometimes with jazzy red stripes on the side. She has the ability to change between white and yellow over a matter of days. Her appearance is decidedly crablike, as she crouches with her two front pairs of angular legs outstretched and hinged forwards. She is at least twice the size of the male, a slender and weedy brown-and-cream creature. She does not weave a web, but she lets out skeins of silk periodically. These act as leads to males during the mating season. She lays her eggs in a pouch made by bending a leaf over backwards and sealing the sides. She guards the eggs and the subsequent hatchlings until they disperse.

25th Walkers along the cliff path in Howth and other warm, rocky parts of the coast near Dublin may be startled by lofty spires of blue blossom. Each has hundreds of individual flowers and can shoot three or four metres into the sky. Honeybees and bumblebees are a constant presence, nuzzling the blooms. This is the giant echium, a native of the Canary Islands. In these coastal locations, *Echium pininana* enjoys a classification almost as long as its flower stalk: it is an ergasiophygophyte, a formerly cultivated plant that has escaped into the wild. Some of the original colonisers on the south-facing flank of Howth came from Earlscliffe, the garden of the late David Robinson, a horticulturist who famously planted many tender species in his favoured acreage. At Killiney, on the far side of Dublin Bay, the dusty leaves of silver ragwort punctuate the cliffs above the beach. These are the offspring of a packet of seed sown around 1875 by the residents of Sorrento Cottage.

26th Now that winter-visiting waders have returned north to breed, coastal sands and mudflats are populated by lesser numbers of birds. At low tide, it is possible to walk along stretches of strand without causing a disturbance. Even when the tide is out, water continues to lie in many areas, and the shallow dips and pools are colonised by green clouds of slimy gutweed and sea lettuce. There are the remains of sea creatures in the sandy mud: tiny, stranded crabs and the empty shells of bivalves, such as mussels, cockles, tellins and razor clams. Keyhole-shaped indentations and the occasional squirt of water are evidence of live razor clams, safe in their burrows. Wormy coils of sand are made by hidden lugworms. Like earthworms, they feed on organic matter and excrete the excess. Sometimes you see this in action when a sudden spiral of sand erupts mysteriously from beneath the surface.

27th Think of holly, and you probably think of red berries or prickly leaves: the last thing that springs to mind is the flowers. Yet, this native tree is in bloom now with four-petalled white flowers: they are easy to miss, being tiny and relatively sparse. Hollies are dioecious (from the Greek for 'two houses'), meaning that male and female flowers are carried on different plants – with male plants being more floriferous than those of the opposite sex. Female trees can be identified by the green orbs in the flower centres, which will swell to become berries. They are surrounded by four protrusions, the remnants of stamens, which never develop.

Pollen is ferried from powder-tipped, club-like anthers on the males by flies, hoverflies and a range of bees, including honeybees, bumblebees, mining and leaf-cutting bees. In commercial holly orchards, one male is sufficient to fertilise twenty females.

28th One of Ireland's more recent alien invaders is the Asian scarlet lily beetle (*Lilioceris lilii*). It appeared in Northern Ireland in 2002, and in the Republic soon after. It is now a familiar insect on lilies and fritillaries. Adults overwinter in the soil and reappear in spring when the host plants re-emerge. The bright red colouring is a warning to potential predators. The beetles are mating now: each female produces hundreds of eggs (like tiny grains of orange rice), laid in small batches on the undersides of leaves. The larvae have an interesting habit of covering themselves with their own excrement, which acts both as camouflage and deterrent. The native common cardinal beetle (*Pyrochroa serraticornis*) is also bright red, but unlike the lily beetle, which has a black head, it has a red head. It is a predator of other insects, and is sometimes found sunbathing on flowers, trunks and stumps.

29th The main flush of dandelions is over, and their sunny heads have been replaced by ghostly, greyish moons. Each seed is attached to a tiny parachute, a pappus, which sends it off to a new location away from the parent plant. Some of the seeds will never make the flight and will be eaten by birds instead. Goldfinches, bullfinches, greenfinches, siskins and linnets all enjoy the seeds. There are several other yellow composite flowers that look superficially like dandelions. Hawksbeards are common on roadsides: first to flower is the beaked hawksbeard, which bears bouncing sprays of dandelion-esque flowers that unfurl from green, melon-like buds. Other plants adding to the confusion are hawkbits, hawkweeds, cat's-ears, goat's beard and sow thistles. Late June will add nipplewort (with smaller faux-dandelion flowers) to the yellow fray. All attract insects, including different bees, beetles and flies.

30th The first baby house sparrows are about, shimmying their wings while begging for food. In hatchlings, the interior of the bill (the gape) is yellow and funnel-like, showing the parents exactly where to insert food. When the bill is closed, the gape looks as if it is a size too big for the head, giving the infant bird a set of sad-clown lips. By the time a young sparrow leaves the nest, the gape has shrunk, but the down-turned frown persists for a few weeks. Often the father does the feeding, as his mate is sitting on the next clutch of eggs. Male sparrows have dark bills and black bibs, and are more assertive-looking than females. In a good year, a pair of sparrows will hatch three broods of chicks. The 'hedge sparrow', a vernacular name for the dunnock – an unrelated bird – is browner all over and has a more pointed bill (for tweezing up insects and other invertebrates).

31st Bog rosemary is in flower, with tiny pink, bulbous bells. This shrubby little plant is related to heather rather than rosemary, but the evergreen leaves are remarkably similar to those of the Mediterranean native. However, its habitat could not be more different, as it requires permanently damp and acidic ground. It is happiest in raised bogs, and is most frequent in the midlands. Bog rosemary is the county plant of Offaly. The insect-eating, round-leaved sundew (which traps and consumes about one insect a week) usually grows not far away. In some bogs, you may hear the haunting cry of the curlew and the coloratura soprano aria of the skylark. Meadow pipits, which have a 'tseep … tseep … tseep …' song and a rapidly climbing and then parachuting display flight, are easily seen now. The white vents and outer tail feathers of these small beige-and-brown streaked birds are obvious when they take to the wing.

June

1st How many of us remember having had a buttercup held under our chin when we were young 'to see if you like butter'? The shiny flower reflected gold onto our skin, showing our supposed affinity for butter. It also ensured that this was one of the first plants we learned as children. There are several buttercup species in Ireland, but three – all in flower now – are more abundant. In gardens, creeping buttercup (*Ranunculus repens*) is the most common, easily identified by its ground-hugging runners linking one plant to the next. Meadow buttercup (*R. acris*) grows in fields and road verges and is tall (up to a metre), graceful and floriferous. The bulbous buttercup (*R. bulbosus*) inhabits dry, grassy places and dunes, reaching no taller than forty centimetres. The sepals on the underside of the flower look as if they have been peeled back. Buttercups are part of an enormous plant family. Familiar members include anemones, clematis, delphiniums and hellebores.

2nd Pine martens are skittering among the trees in forests and woodland. They are sleek and sinuous, cat-sized animals (the name in Irish is *cat crainn*) with brown fur and a cream-coloured bib on the throat and upper chest. These members of the weasel family are normally secretive, solitary and nocturnal. But in summer, the species is at its most active during daylight hours. The young kits, which are born blind and bald in spring, are making their first forays outside in company with their mothers. Males take no part in kit-care. Summertime is also mating time, although the fertilised eggs are not implanted in the uterus until winter. Pine martens were almost extinct by the twentieth century. Their habitats were destroyed, and they were hunted for fur, and poisoned and persecuted by owners of poultry and game birds. They are now fully protected, and populations are slowly beginning to recover. They are one of the few species that lives in commercial conifer plantations. Their diet is broad: fruits, nuts, small mammals, birds, frogs and invertebrates, including earthworms, ground beetles and snails. It is thought that the increase in pine martens is helping control invasive grey squirrels, and thus aid the recovery of the native red squirrel population. The reasons are unclear, but it may be that the reds are more nimble and more attuned to pine martens as predators. It may also be that grey squirrels are stressed by the presence of pine martens and therefore fail to thrive.

3rd Beech trees are in flower. The slightest breeze brings the lightweight, spent blossom floating gently downwards, like gold-tinged snowflakes. The male catkins remain intact and carpet the ground under the trees with tiny little pompoms threaded through with knobbly anthers.

Scattered among the fluffy debris are curved brown scales, the discarded coverings of buds. Beech belongs to the same family as the oak; both take decades to mature and to flower with any conviction. Some years beech produces few flowers and few nuts. The trees bloom most prolifically following a hot, dry summer. A profusion of spring flowers may lead to a 'mast year' – an abundance of seeds – if the right weather conditions prevail over the following months. Ash trees, the last to produce foliage, are finally clothing themselves with leaves. Conifers are pushing out new needles, soft lime-green shoots on the ends of all their branches.

4th The treecreeper is resident across two-thirds of the landmass of Ireland – anywhere that there is a concentration of trees for it to creep on. The little bird does not call attention to itself as it searches for spiders and small insects in crevices. The mottled brown-and-grey plumage on its back camouflages it against the bark of most trees, and its spiralling upwards progress ensures that it is usually disappearing around the far side of a trunk when you spot it. Long, spidery toes grip the bark, while a stiff tail helps to ratchet it up the tree. Its curved needle of a bill quickly probes for invertebrates. When a bird has climbed up one trunk, it drops down to the next tree and works its way up. Parents are feeding chicks now, so are busy foraging for invertebrates. In old estates, treecreepers hollow out the spongy bark of giant redwoods (*Sequoiadendron*) to create roosting cavities.

5th Saint Patrick's cabbage is in flower. This little saxifrage is daintily pretty in all its parts. A low rosette of spoon-shaped, serrated leaves sprouts wiry stems of white, pink-freckled flowers, each crowned with a filigree of rose-toned stamens. *Saxifraga spathularis* is a member of our Lusitanian flora, a select group of fifteen Mediterranean species that occur both in Ireland (usually the west and south) and in northern Spain and Portugal. This curious distribution has not been convincingly explained. *Cabáiste an mhadra rua* (fox's cabbage) grows on acid rocks, including old stone walls, often presenting itself preciously from among cushions of moss. The saxifrage name comes from the Latin words *saxum* and *frango*, meaning rock and break, as the plant, which often grows in crevices, was believed to be capable of breaking rocks. It is found mostly in a line from Cork to Donegal (skipping the Burren) and is abundant in places. An incongruous colony on Lugnaquilla in the Wicklow Mountains, discovered in 1924, is an interesting anomaly. Strangely, there is little folklore attached to the plant, although it was recommended as a cure for cuts in County Cork and for rheumatism in County Mayo.

6th There are twenty-one native bumblebees in Ireland, and the different species can be difficult to identify. All that fur and all those stripe formations can easily merge into a vague classification of 'some kind of *Bombus*'. The Latin name means buzzing or booming, and is pleasingly onomatopoeic. In English, it was once the 'humble-bee', which may refer to its nesting in low places: in holes in the ground or at the base of plants. Seventeen of our species are social bumblebees, building up colonies of fifty to four hundred individuals by mid-summer. The other four species are cuckoo bees: a female lays her eggs in the nest of similar-looking social bees, and her young are reared by the unwitting workers. In parks and gardens the easiest bumblebee to identify is *Bombus lapidarius*, the red-tailed bumblebee – jet-black and velvety with a red rump. There is a copycat cuckoo bee, but it is less common.

7th Yellow rattle is starting to bloom in meadows and grasslands. The small flowers emerge from swollen calyxes, and look like minuscule yellow jack-in-the-boxes. When the flowers fade and the plants dry, the seeds rattle inside their containers, and give the plant its name. It is a hemiparasitic plant: although it has green leaves that photosynthesise, its roots latch onto the roots of grass, and steal some of the nutrition. It is a valuable component of wildflower meadows, as it decreases competition from grasses. In times past, farmers disliked it, as it reduced hay yield by as much as 50 per cent. Eyebright is another pilfering plant. It inhabits damp acidic ground, such as pastures and heaths. Its tiny flowers are white to pale lilac, and are lined with purple nectar guides. A hand lens reveals an egg-yolk-yellow throat. It was widely used in folk medicine to soothe eye ailments, including styes, conjunctivitis and inflammations. Two other hemiparasitic plants are lousewort (of marshes, meadows and bogs) and red bartsia (of grasslands and roadsides). Both have pink, tubular and hooded flowers.

8th The first brood of baby robins is out and about. They are the same build and size as their parents, but they lack the red breast. Instead, they wear a speckled brown suit of feathers, like a rusty-toned, country tweed. Their bright, beady eyes are unmistakable. Before the juveniles emerge into the wider world, adult robins can be seen busily picking near-invisible insects and their larvae off plants and darting into undergrowth or dense foliage to feed the concealed fledglings. Young robins are not shy, and like their parents, will follow a gardener around, hoping that invertebrates will be turned up when the soil is dug. Robins in other parts of Europe are more wary of humans and tend to stick to the cover of woodlands. One theory is that they are cautious because they are exposed to hunters and trappers at the southern end of their range. Along with many garden birds, robins have a high death rate in their first year. Natural predators and domestic cats account for the demise of many juveniles. The average lifespan is 1.1 years, but those that survive that critical point may live for considerably longer. The oldest known robin, in the Czech Republic, was nineteen years and four months.

9th Ragwort is in bloom and will continue to put out its sunny yellow daisies for months. It is a much-maligned wildflower. Although it can be toxic to livestock, many animals know enough to avoid it. Poisoning happens most often when it is eaten unwittingly in fodder, or when animals are kept in pastures with poor grazing. It is a superb plant for insects: over its five- or six-month flowering period it sustains numerous species of bee, fly (including hoverflies), wasp, beetle, butterfly and moth. Often the leaves and flowers are covered in caterpillars, neatly striped in the black and amber tones of Kilkenny's county colours. These are the larvae of its most dazzling dependent, the day-flying cinnabar moth. As an adult, this moth emerges as a County Down supporter, with wings strikingly marked in red and black. The British poet Frances Cornford (granddaughter of Charles Darwin) celebrated this native plant wholeheartedly:

The ragworts, growing up so straight,
Are emperors who stand in state,
And march about, so proud and bold,
In crowns of fairy-story gold.

10th Greenfly, or aphids, to give them their correct name, are in their early summer population boom. They congregate on the softest tissue of plants, the new growth at the tips of shoots. Ants have a special relationship with these sap-sucking insects: they 'farm' them in order to collect the honeydew (waste sap) that their little livestock produce. They 'milk' the aphids by stroking and patting their backs with their antennae until they produce a drop of sugary liquid – a bit like burping a baby. Ants protect their herds from predators such as ladybirds, and they sometimes carry individuals to newer pastures and even into their nests. There is evidence that certain kinds of aphids are capable of turning the tables in an act of aggressive mimicry. They are able to imitate the creamy blobbiness of ant larvae, leading the ants to place them carefully next to their own immature offspring. Once there, the aphids pierce the larval skin and suck out their vital fluids.

11th Elder trees and shrubs are beginning to flower, producing flat clouds of tiny, five-petalled florets that emit a citrusy, grassy, many-layered perfume. The species is useful to all manner of fauna (including humans) in all its seasons. The flowers are visited by many insects, and the fruit is an important food for birds in autumn. At least half a dozen moth species lay their eggs on it so that the caterpillars may feed on the leaves. The most beautiful is the large, lemon-yellow swallow-tailed moth, which appears next month. It is a nocturnal insect, so it is not often seen, except by those who use moth traps. The caterpillars mimic brown twigs. Ground elder is an unrelated plant, belonging to the carrot family, but its leaves look roughly similar. While elder is a native plant, ground elder was introduced. It is believed to have been brought to Britain by the Romans, and it arrived here afterwards.

12th Urban gardens are alive with the clamorous cries of starlings begging incessantly for food. Baby starlings are the same size and shape as adults, but instead of the shiny, speckled suits of their parents, they wear plumage that is matte and dull brown. The eyes appear dark and cavernous, giving the birds an unsettling, gothic look. Soon the parents will abandon the youngsters to go off and raise a second brood. First-year breeding females often act as cuckoos, removing an egg from an established starling nest and laying one of her own in its place. When young, the starling's repertoire is limited to screeching, food-seeking calls, but as an adult its range expands to virtuosic melodies incorporating clicks, whistles and chatters. Starlings are accomplished mimics, able to produce credible imitations not just of other birds, but of car alarms, mobile ringtones and other modern devices. Sound recordist Chris Watson captured starlings in the Inner Hebrides imitating the hiccuppy stages of an old-fashioned, two-stroke engine starting up. The recording was made adjacent to a long-abandoned, rusting heap of an engine, which suggests that the melody had been passed down through many generations of birds.

13th Ireland's waterways are at their busiest now, with plants in flower and wildfowl minding their hatchlings. In Dublin, the two canals flow like watery ribbons of diversity through the capital. Flag iris, our only native iris, is brandishing its clear yellow blooms along the margins. Each flower is loaded with nectar: a Bristol University study showed that *Iris pseudacorus* produces more sugar per flower per day than any other native plant. Meadowsweet is producing its first, frothy white flowers. Common reed – the plant used for thatching – still wears seed-heads from last year, while the new leaves push up from below. Moorhens make nests among reeds and rushes, often incorporating bits of plastic into the structure. Parents and chicks can be seen making quick forays from the cover of vegetation. Mallards are braver, trailing their ducklings behind as they swim in the open water. A small number of mute swans nest on Dublin's canal banks. Although less noisy than the whooper swans that visit wetlands in winter, they are by no means mute.

14th

The horny-goloch is an awesome beast,
Soople and scaly;
It has twa horns, an a hantle o feet,
An a forkie tailie.

The creature in the Scottish rhyme is an earwig, and seen up close it is indeed an awesome beast. Just as awe-inspiring, perhaps, is the fact that unlike many insects, earwigs do not have larval and pupal stages. Instead, they hatch as pale mini-earwigs – nymphs – and go through a series of five moults before reaching adulthood. Mother earwigs guard their eggs and infant offspring, leaving them to their own devices only after the second moult. Each time they shed their old skins, they are creamy-coloured and ghostly, but they darken within a few hours. Immature horny-golochs are about now, and can often be found concealed under plant pots or in crevices. Although it is a myth that earwigs like to hide in one's ears, there are still plenty of remedies for coaxing them out, should they seek refuge there. A strawberry or a baked apple pressed against the ear was supposed to attract them, as would a cup of hot water placed nearby.

15th Common hogweed is in flower along roadsides and hedgerows. It has taken over from its earlier-blooming relative, cow parsley. Hogweed has similar white umbrellas of blossom, which attract bees, flies, beetles and other insects. Its nectar production is prodigious. It is much coarser and taller than cow parsley, and can reach two metres and more. Short, bristly hairs cover the plant, while the broad, intricate leaves look as if they have been folded and cut out with scissors. Giant hogweed is at least twice the size of our native species, and is impossible to miss. Gargantuan in all its parts, a mature specimen can top five metres. It was introduced from the Caucasus in the nineteenth century, and is often seen along river banks. J. C. Loudon, the Scots botanist and garden taste-maker, wrote in 1836 that he had given seeds of the 'magnificent umbelliferous plant' to a friend who was touring Ireland. Some of today's plants are probably the descendants of his gift. The seeds, which remain viable for up to fifteen years, float on the water, producing new plants when they are washed up. The sap of giant hogweed contains chemical compounds known as furanocoumarins which can cause serious skin inflammations, especially in combination with sunlight.

16th The warmer weather in this month makes walking on beaches and strands at low tide a pleasure. Clusters of rock jut up from the sand in the intertidal zone – the area that is alternately submerged and exposed as the tides shift. Rocks are sometimes encrusted with barnacles and limpets, giving them a rough and grainy texture. Colonies of blue mussels, sometimes in the thousands, cover parts of the surface. They cling to the rock and to each other using byssus threads, strong filaments that act as guy-ropes. Juvenile mussels may seek protection in empty barnacle shells. As they mature, the mussels' own shells become home to live barnacles. Mussels are filter feeders, taking their nutrition from minute particles in the water that they inhale and exhale when they are submerged. A mature mussel can filter two to three litres of water per hour. In the intertidal sector, some rocks are almost completely dressed in seaweeds, mostly wracks. Rock pools and damp crevices hold anemones, starfish, dog whelks and crabs. Crabs and starfish often shelter under boulders, remaining immobile in order to conserve moisture.

17th During hot days at the seaside, one plant you don't want to encounter with bare feet is sea holly – an inhabitant of sand dunes and beach margins. Usually no more than thirty centimetres high, *Eryngium maritimum* is prickly all over and thistle-like in its appearance and ability to inflict pain. Despite the spiny look, it belongs to *Apiaceae*, the same family that gives us carrot, parsley and hogweed. Its taproot is immensely long, drilling a metre or more into the sand where it seeks moisture and acts as an anchor in the unstable ground. Leaves, stems and bracts are covered with a waxy, blue-green coating, resistant to salt, wind and abrasive sand. The flowers, appearing now, are a cone-shaped cluster of deep maritime blue. Its roots were believed to have aphrodisiac properties: in Shakespeare's *Merry Wives of Windsor*, Falstaff, in a frenzy of lust, bids the sky to 'snow eringoes'. A less common coastal plant is the yellow horned poppy (*Glaucium flavum*) with silky-petalled yellow flowers borne over greenish-grey, bristly, fleshy foliage. After the flowers fade, the ovaries elongate to form whippy, curving seedpods, up to thirty centimetres, and more like tentacles than horns.

18th Many garden birds are engrossed in feeding and protecting their young now. Their entire day is a continual round of hunting and foraging, making deliveries and dealing with potential predators or intruders. Not so the wood pigeon. Although they may raise up to three broods in a season, pairs can often be seen leisurely canoodling, or as the ornithologists call it, allopreening. Mated birds sit closely together and groom their partner's neck and head, an action that helps to reinforce the pair-bond while also removing hard-to-reach parasites. In the evening, individual birds often hunch on top of chimneys and lamp posts, looking not unlike resting sparrowhawks. Wood pigeons start to breed early in the year and continue into August or September. Both parents take turns incubating the eggs (males take shorter turns) and both feed the chicks on 'crop milk'. This is a curd-like substance manufactured by specialised cells lining the crop, a muscular pouch in the bird's neck. It is highly nutritious, containing more protein and fat than either cow or human milk.

19th Look up at the chimneys around you and before long you'll see one with a plant growing out of it. Most abundant is buddleja, with its squirrel tails of purple flowers. The butterfly bush, as it is also known, was introduced here at the end of the nineteenth century, but it soon jumped from gardens into wasteland, cracks in masonry and disused chimney pots. Each raceme (long cluster) of flower produces thousands of lightweight seeds. These have long wings on either side, which whisk them through the air on the slightest breeze. In its native territories of Sichuan and Hubei provinces in China, buddleja grows on shingle by streams, in scrubland and on roadside cliffs – so it is perfectly at home in the lofty quarters of our rooftops. The New Zealand cordyline also occasionally inhabits the same spaces in our urban landscapes. Its seeds were deposited there by birds that gorged on the pale, waxy fruits.

20th Greenbottles are in many parks, gardens and fields – not empty wine or beer bottles, but flies of the *Lucilia* genus. They are handsome insects with a glossy, metallic sheen to their bodies. The most common of these is *L. sericata*, but it is impossible to positively identify without a microscope. It is a species that is loathed by farmers, yet admired by the medical profession. Both have good reasons. Greenbottles cause 'flystrike' in sheep: adult flies lay eggs on wet, soiled wool and the resulting maggots infest lesions on the sheep's skin. Paradoxically, this is the same fly species that is used in MDT or 'maggot debridement therapy' in humans. Sterile maggots are applied to necrotic tissue in wounds, and they eat away the dead material. They also exude substances that kill bacteria, including MRSA (methicillin-resistant *Staphylococcus aureus*). This is a rare case of where you want a fly in the ointment.

21st In *A Midsummer Night's Dream*, Titania, queen of the fairies, sleeps on a 'bank where the wild thyme blows, / Where oxlips and the nodding violet grows, / Quite over-canopied with luscious woodbine, / With sweet musk-roses and with eglantine.' Woodbine is honeysuckle, while eglantine is sweet briar, a thorny rose with scented foliage. All the above are still common enough, except oxlip, which is confined to a small part of eastern England. Wildflowers popped up continually in Shakespeare's writings. His potential floral palette was limited compared to what it would be today. Since his time, in Ireland alone, several hundred alien plants have set up home. Ornamentals have leapt over garden walls and floated down streams, other species have hitched lifts on ships. A modern Titania would perhaps sleep on 'a bank where slender speedwell blows, where winter heliotrope's huge leaf grows, quite over-canopied with giant hogweed, with traveller's joy and flying ragwort seed'.

22nd The rock pipit looks like a miniature thrush with blurred and dusty markings. Duller and slightly larger than the meadow pipit, it lives only along the coast and is more frequent on the west side of the country. As Richard J. Ussher and Robert Warren put it in their *Birds of Ireland* (published in 1900): 'It enlivens the most awful cliffs with its simple notes and easy movements.' One of the vernacular names is the shore lark (not to be confused with the real shore lark, a rare European visitor to Ireland), while in parts of Connaught it is *circín trágha*, the beach chicken. At this time of the year, rock pipits are found around harbours and other rocky areas, where they make their nests in crevices, usually near the ground. They are busy raising their young now. Some of these are still in the nest, while others are making their first awkward attempts at independence, bumbling against rocks and pier walls as they try to gain a foothold. Adults are looking somewhat threadbare at present, as their plumage has been abraded by salt-laden winds, sand and rocks, and bleached by the high light levels of the seaside. Soon they will moult and grow a spanking new set of feathers.

23rd Our two native water lilies are in bloom, decorating canals and lakes with their beauteous art nouveau leaves and flowers. (While we're on the subject of art, the Impressionist master of water lilies, Claude Monet, mainly painted new hybrids rather than wild ones. They were raised by his breeder friend, a lawyer named Joseph Bory Latour-Marliac.) In Ireland, *Nuphar lutea*, with its yellow ping-pong-ball flowers, is the more common water lily. It occurs mostly in the northern and eastern parts of the country, and is the water lily of Dublin's canals. Its blooms smell like alcohol, giving it the common name of 'brandy bottle'. The odour is said to attract small flies, which act as pollinators. The resulting seeds are covered in a buoyant jelly-like substance, which allows them to float to a new location. After about three days, the jelly breaks down and the seeds drop to the mud below. The yellow water lily's white cousin (*Nymphaea alba*) is more often found in the west and south (especially Cork, Kerry, Galway and Mayo), although it also grows in some Wicklow lakes.

24th The grey squirrel is one of Ireland's more visible alien invaders. Famously, the Irish population of this North American rodent are descendants of a wedding gift that arrived in Castle Forbes in County Longford in 1911. A dozen, packaged in a wicker basket, were presented by the Duke of Buckingham. When the lid was opened, off they scampered, to merrily wreak havoc in their newly adopted country. Over the decades, the Americans have moved over much of the island, although rarely straying west of the Shannon. They are twice the size of the native red squirrel and have a more robust digestive system. The greys are able to eat nuts before they are ripe, thus depriving the reds of their food. They have also done untold damage to tree plantations, stripping the bark of broad-leaved trees to get at the rising sap underneath. Culling has reduced numbers, and in counties where the pine marten is recovering, the greys are waning. In summer, they often have a russet tone to their dorsal fur, but their size and tuft-less ears make them unmistakable.

25th Red valerian (*Centranthus ruber*) sprouts cheerfully from dry places all over Ireland. The fleshy-rooted perennial pops out of the crevices in stone walls, colonises dry banks and embellishes abandoned buildings with its showy panicles of flower all summer long. They are more often pink or white than true red. It is so ubiquitous along train tracks that it has earned the common name of railway weed. Its seeds have weeny shuttlecock feathers and are easily whisked along to newer quarters by passing trains. The Mediterranean alien was introduced to these islands over four hundred years ago, probably as an ornamental. John Gerard wrote in his 1597 *Herball* that it 'groweth plentifully in my garden, being a great ornament to the same, and not common in England'. The tiny flowers have relatively long tubes and attract insects with long proboscses, such as certain butterflies and the exotic-looking hummingbird hawk-moth, which occasionally uses it as a place to deposit its eggs. The medicinal valerian of sleeping potions is a different species, the native *Valeriana officinalis* – a pale-pink flowered plant that is now less common than its interloping relative.

26th The harbour porpoise is Ireland's smallest cetacean (the group of sea mammals that includes whales, dolphins and porpoises), averaging about 1.5 metres in length. It is also the most common of the twenty-five that inhabit our waters. Numbers are difficult to estimate: there are definitely tens of thousands, but they are usually visible only as single individuals or pairs on calm days with a flat sea. They are present all along the coastline, with the highest counts between Howth Head and Dalkey in County Dublin. Dún Laoghaire pier and a comfortable, coast-side seat on the Dart offer good sighting opportunities. Look for a dark form that curls sinuously out of the water, barely breaking the surface, quite unlike the athletic leaping of dolphins. The short, triangular dorsal fin midway along the back is the diagnostic feature. At one time *an muc mhara* – the sea pig – as it is known in Irish, was eaten, but now it, and all cetaceans, are protected in Irish waters. Special Areas of Conservation (SAC) have been designated for the harbour porpoise:

the Blasket Islands, Roaring Water Bay and the Rockabill to Dalkey Island SAC.

27th Common nettle is in bloom, with pale green, branched tassels sprouting from the junction between leaf and stem. Male and female flowers are carried on different plants: the latter are recognisable by their slightly furred appearance, as if they have been touched by frost. This effect is from the minute tufts on the tiny stigmas, designed to catch grains of windborne pollen that have been ejected by male flowers. *Urtica dioica* (*neantóg* in Irish) is perennial, and can grow to a metre or more, putting it at just the right height to sting the vulnerable skin between back of wrist and inner elbow. It has a nastier sting than its shorter annual relative, *U. urens* (*neantóg bheag*). Peacock, red admiral, small tortoiseshell and painted lady butterflies lay their eggs on common nettle. Recent resident, the comma, also deposits her eggs, singly, often on the leaf tips, like minuscule decorative beads. In folk medicine, nettles were used in many remedies, including as a cure for measles and a potion for purifying the blood.

28th Barn owls are more likely to nest in ruins, neglected outbuildings and tree cavities than in the busy, industrial barns of today. We are in the peak of the breeding season now. The chicks (up to five in a good year) perform a loud, hissing, food-begging call that sounds like an espresso machine in a busy coffee shop. Adults have an other-worldly shriek, traditionally associated with the call of the banshee. The Irish name is *scréachóg reilige*, the graveyard screecher. The barn owl is a marvel of adaptation: wing tips are fringed to allow silent flight; claws are modified to open widely to easily scoop up hapless animals; and the heart-shaped, concave face is an efficient sound collector. Rats, mice and shrews are its main prey. The species is red-listed (of highest conservation concern); issues include habitat loss and secondary poisoning from rodenticides. GPS trackers on foraging barn owls have shown that they avoid areas of intensive agriculture and hunt mostly along hedgerows and grassy margins and in rough grassland. There are perhaps only five hundred breeding pairs in the Republic of Ireland.

29th Worker wasps are beginning to appear. These are sterile females, the first offspring of the queens who mated last autumn, hibernated over winter and emerged in spring. During late spring and early summer, each queen concentrates on finding a suitable place, building a paper nest from wood (scraped from dried plant matter, fence posts and the like), laying eggs and raising the larvae. She is eclectic in her choice of location: perhaps a garden shed, the eaves of a house, an old animal burrow or a hole in a tree. Her daughter workers are now taking over the work of expanding and maintaining the nest structure, foraging for food (insects and spiders) and tending to the larvae. The workers mash up the invertebrates before feeding them to their charges. As a reward, the larvae secrete a sugary saliva: this ensures they are not eaten by their nursemaids. The exchange is known as trophallaxis.

30th Meadow buttercup is at its loveliest, raising its chrome yellow flowers on wiry, widely branched stems. A whole field speckled with it is an unforgettable and uplifting sight, a summer memory to be kept safe for darker days. With many local authorities now managing parkland as traditional meadow, these nostalgic landscapes are returning to our suburbs. Red and white clovers attract bumblebees; some ribwort plantains still sport tattered halos of stamens and dock raises its red-brown spires. Common mouse-ear is easy to miss, with its minute white petals making barely-there sparks of light. Grasses are in flower also: soft, cylindrical spikes of foxtails and timothy, loose panicles of bents, neatly engineered and regular crested dog's-tail and a waving, swaying crowd of other grain-tips in shades from palest grey-green to deep wine. Overhead, a kestrel may hover, searching for small rodents in the grass.

July

1st The beadlet anemone is common in rock pools in the upper tidal zone, a magical habitat that is revealed at low tide. Creatures that live here are robust species, able to tolerate exposure to air and to the changing levels of salt in the water (it becomes more saline through evaporation in hot weather). When the tide recedes and *Actinia equina* is exposed, it tightens into a dense, dark-red blob, like a blood clot on the side of a rock. Yet, when submerged, it blossoms into a startlingly beautiful, tentacled crown, bejewelled with a circle of violet beads. These are sacs filled with explosive, poison-tipped tendrils, which it uses to sting prey and defend territory from other, unrelated beadlet anemones. Its tentacles whoosh food into the central orifice, the gastrovascular cavity. A while later, waste matter is expelled from the same opening. John Rutty gives the rather nice name '*Champignon de la mer*' in his 1772 work, *An Essay towards the Natural History of the County of Dublin*: 'it resembles a mushroom when shut, but becomes like a flower of an *Anemone* when it opens its horns...'

2nd Hedge mustard is an opportunist that inserts itself wherever there is a niche in our man-made landscape. It grows in hedgerows, on field margins and wasteland, and wedged into the crevices alongside roads, pavements and walls. Despite its ubiquity, this angular, gangly plant is easily missed, as it is 'weedy' and lacklustre, with upright, wiry stems sparsely clad in leaves resembling those of rocket. Minute, four-petalled, pale-yellow flowers are borne on gradually elongating stalks that eventually form a fragile candelabra. Once you notice *Sisymbrium officinale*, you see it everywhere: on average, a plant on waste ground produces over four thousand seeds. The *officinale* epithet denotes that it was once a medicinal herb. Its uses were legion: it was an antidote to poison and a remedy for worms, swellings, sciatica, incontinence and hoarseness. Other plants that enjoy infertile soil and arid conditions often pop up alongside it: tiny tufts of meadow grass; wall barley, with feathery, green flower heads; pink-tipped, broad-leaved willowherb; little sprawls of chickweed. Also here are groundsel, dandelion, herb Robert, sow thistle, plantain, spurge and wood avens. Pineapple weed, introduced over a century ago from North America in poultry feed, is another such plant.

3rd   Social media feeds are full of pictures of the six-spot burnet moth: a beautifully designed insect with a scattering of crimson dots on its shiny, blue-black wings. A pair of black, hockey-stick antennae add to the appeal of this daytime-flying moth, which is common at present in coastal grasslands, especially in sunny weather. It is gratifyingly easy to photograph, as the moth is slow to move when it is sipping nectar, or indeed, mating. When it flies, with its characteristic unhurried pace, it produces a noticeable buzz. The larvae of *Zygaena filipendulae* feed on common bird's-foot trefoil (and occasionally on greater bird's-foot trefoil, clover and kidney vetch), and hibernate over winter in sheltered spots near the ground. They wake up in spring, feed some more, and then pupate in yellow, papery cocoons, attached to grasses. Adults emerge in June and July. The bright colouring is a warning to predators to keep away: the six-spot burnet moth contains cyanide.

4th   Visit a boggy place in Cork and Kerry now and you may encounter the large-flowered butterwort in bloom. The flowers are borne singly on long stalks and look almost like violets – with purple petals and a tail-like spur at the back. One of the common names is bog violet. The pretty, richly toned flowers look incongruous, sprouting from a basal rosette of pallid, rubbery-looking leaves with curled edges. If it were an ordinary plant, such off-colour, flabby foliage would have you thinking it was sickly and undernourished. But butterworts are not ordinary and are not fuelled only by nutrients in the soil. Instead, they supplement their diet with insects. When a tiny fly, beetle or ant steps on to a leaf, the plant discharges an acid which digests the insect in a number of days. Common butterwort and pale butterwort are two other native species of *Pinguicula*. They are more widespread, but not as showy.

5th Warm summer nights, when all the windows are open, often bring an explosion of animal sounds into the house. This year's fox cubs, which were conceived in late winter and early spring, are getting comfortable with their new surroundings. Like their parents, they are largely nocturnal. Their interactions can be noisy: a torrent of sharp barks, squeals, chitters, chirps, squeaks, squalls and mews. Most of these vocalisations are exclusive to cubs. Occasionally they emit bursts of staccato, machine-gun-like 'gekkering'. This accompanies play-fighting, practice for later on when rival males meet and sort out who gets the vixen. Another summer utterance is the alarm call of the adults that have helped to raise the young. This is a shortened, less forlorn version of the blood-chilling shriek of wintertime when courting pairs are calling to each other. In autumn, the young males will leave and seek out new territories.

6th Foxglove, or *lus mór*, grows in every county. The deep pink (and occasionally white) bells have prompted at least two dozen vernacular names in Ireland, including fairy cap, fairy gloves, fairy thimbles and fairy bells. In Ulster, the names blob, cottagers and dead man's fingers are used, among others. *Digitalis purpurea* is the source of various cardiac medications, and is documented as a traditional remedy in Ireland for heart complaints. The stimulants contained in it are extremely potent, so doses were sometimes lethal rather than therapeutic. Another common name, throat-wort, describes its use as a cure for sore throats. Each foxglove flower produces thousands of tiny seeds, smaller than the finest grain of salt. They are light enough to be blown on the wind. Dispersal is helped by the tall flower stems, which launch them from a height. Foxgloves often appear as if by magic in newly cleared ground because seeds remain viable for many years in soil, and germinate upon exposure to light. The garden and common carder bumblebees (*Bombus hortorum* and *B. pascuorum*) are the foxglove's principal pollinators: both have long tongues that are able to reach into the deep corolla tubes. Carder bees collect moss and bits of grass that they 'card' (comb out) into a covering for their nests.

7th Meadow browns are beginning to emerge from their pupae, where they have been quietly metamorphosing from lightly furred, green caterpillars. The butterflies are mainly brown, with eye spots in orange patches on the forewings. They are one of our most widespread butterflies, flitting busily over meadows and rough grasslands. Look for them also over the long grass at the edges of fields and roads. Only one generation is produced per year, with the eggs hatching between late summer and autumn. The larval phase can span eight months. During winter the caterpillars are in semi-hibernation, rousing on mild days to feed on grasses. In late spring they enter the pupal stage, which lasts three to four weeks. Adult butterflies may be on the wing between now and early October. They take nectar from bramble, thistles, knapweed, scabious, buttercups, ragwort, yarrow and other plants. Males are more active than the females, fluttering low over vegetation looking for mates and checking out the competition. Meadow browns have been known to mate with other butterfly species, but without success.

8th Bog cotton – or cotton grass, as it is known to botanists – is in full fluffy display. The snow-white, silken tufts that bob and shimmer over bogs and heathland are the seedheads of the flowers that bloomed in spring. You would be forgiven for not noticing the flowers, as they are nondescript straw-coloured entities, a feature of many members of the sedge family. The flowers lack colour, as they are wind-pollinated, and have no need to attract insects. The seeds also depend on the wind for their dispersal. Unlike dandelions, which lose their parachuted seeds over a matter of days, *Eriophorum* species hold on to their puffy pappi for months. In times past, bog cotton (*ceannbhán* in Irish, meaning 'white head') was recommended as a cure for burns and for worms in children. Reportedly, it was used as a dressing for wounds in the First World War. Bog asphodel, which bears clusters of yellow stars on long stalks, often grows in the same habitat, as do heather, ling and cross-leaved heath.

9th If you're walking in the mountains, or near steep cliffs, or where there are lofty ruins, listen for the rusty 'crawk! crawk!' of the raven. The largest member of the crow family is not hard to spot. With a wingspan of up to 1.5 metres, it is an accomplished flier, soaring gracefully and performing acrobatic tumbles and turns. Breeding pairs are monogamous, and may return to the same nesting site year after year, often under an overhang on the rock face. Four to six eggs are laid, and young ravens stay within their parents for several weeks after fledging. Ravens are long-lived: the oldest known wild individual, in Norway, was over twenty-three years old. *Fiach dubh*, as it is known in Irish, is the subject of grim superstitions and folk tales. One story, told in Drogheda, has a habitual drunk forgetting everything, including where he lived, after hearing the raven's voice. It was widely believed that a raven flying near, or even into a house, presaged a death in the home.

10th Among our thirty native orchid species, one of the most frequently seen is the common spotted orchid, *Dactylorhiza fuchsii* subsp. *fuchsii*. Its ankle- to knee-high stalks carry pink spikes of densely clustered flowers, and are clearly visible in a mixed bag of habitats: grassland, roadsides, marshes, woodland and dune 'slacks' – the low-lying depressions near the water table in dune systems. It is usually easily identified by its tripartite labellum (the lower lip) with the central point longer than the two outer ones. The spur points downward. The spots in the common name refer to the liver-toned patches often found on the leaves. The flowers, which vary from white to dark pink, are delicately marked with darker streaks and dots. Pyramidal orchids (*Anacamptis pyramidalis*) are also in bloom in similar locations, although not in damp soils. They are one of the most common roadside orchids. The magenta flowers are arranged into clusters that are most pointy and pyramidal before all the flowers have opened.

11th We have eleven damselfly and seventeen dragonfly species breeding here, while a handful of other visitors occasionally pop in. The presence of these elite insects, collectively known as *Odonata*, can be an indicator of water quality, as all spend their early life as aquatic larvae. Unpolluted water is essential, as this nymph stage is lengthy, lasting from two to three months for the emerald damselfly and over five years for the golden-ringed dragonfly. All are in flight now, except for the migrant hawker dragonfly, which will be appearing in a few weeks. Damselflies are small and dainty insects, needle-thin and between three and four centimetres long. All hold their wings closed or partially closed while at rest. The six blue damselflies, which are bestowed with an astonishing, neon luminance, are the most obvious, with the blue-tailed (*Ischnura elegans*) and common blue (*Enallagma cyathigerum*) being the most often recorded. Dragonflies are larger and stockier, and spread their two pairs of wings when stationary. An identification swatch for Ireland's dragonflies is available from biodiversityireland.ie/shop

12th Roadsides in the west and southwest are hung with the crimson-and-plum bells of fuchsia. Most fuchsia shrubs and hedges were planted intentionally, although a few are naturalised, having sprung from detached or discarded material. Fuchsia is 'self-layering' also, putting out roots where stems are blown or bent over to touch the ground. Although its flower is the emblem of West Cork, *Fuchsia magellanica* is a native of Chile and Argentina. The cultivar most often seen is 'Riccartonii': it was raised by Mr Young, the head gardener at Riccarton estate, near Edinburgh, around 1830. *Deora Dé* (meaning tears of God in Irish) is popular with bumblebees. If you snap off the ovary at the top, you can taste the tiny drops of nectar for yourself. And, if you have children in tow, you can take another flower and make a tiny, full-skirted ballerina. Gently remove the stigma along with six of the eight dangling stamens to leave just two, which then become her legs.

13th Summer days see an influx of jellyfish at seaside bathing places. Several different species turn up at our coasts. The common or moon jellyfish (*Aurelia aurita*) is the most frequent: it has four rings at its centre, a little like a stemless four-leaf clover. The compass jellyfish (*Chrysaora hysoscella*) has brown spoke-like markings radiating from the hub. The blue jellyfish (*Cyanea lamarckii*) is rare-ish, while its relative, the lion's mane (*C. capillata*) is becoming increasingly widespread along the coast. The name of the latter comes from the mane-like mass of frilled and tangled arms, yellow-russet to deep purple, that dangle from beneath its bell. It is the largest known jellyfish: the greatest recorded bell size was 2.3 metres, on a specimen washed up on a Massachusetts shore in 1870. The tentacles were thirty-seven metres long. Lion's mane can look like a mass of free-floating seaweed, but if you watch it for a minute, you'll see that, unlike seaweed, which stays on the surface, the jellyfish sinks and rises. The Irish for jellyfish is *smugairle róin*, which translates as seal spittle.

14th July is often a droughty month, a month that sees grass become brittle and sere. White clover is unloved by lawn fiends, but it has far more stamina than grass. Its leaves remain fresh in very dry conditions and are often the only green thing in otherwise brown lawns. Clover and other leguminous species (members of the pea family) form a partnership with bacteria, which live in nodules on the roots. The bacteria take nitrogen gas from air pockets in the soil and convert it into nitrates, which are usable by plants. Clovers provide food for the caterpillars of the clouded yellow butterfly and for those of four moth species. The individual florets of white clover are shallow, allowing many insects to reach the nectar: among them are honeybees, bumblebees and tiny parasitoid wasps. White clover (*Trifolium repens*) is one of the plants that was traditionally claimed to be the 'real' shamrock, although it is the related yellow clover which is now grown commercially.

15th Species that are new to Ireland often turn up first in County Wexford, perhaps because the winds favour it, the terrain is congenial and the weather is relatively sunny. The county also has many eagle-eyed naturalists keeping vigil. Magpies are one of the earliest documented new arrivals. According to a 1682 report by Colonel Solomon Richards, 'there came with a strong blacke Easterly wind, a flight of Magpies, under a dozen ... out of England, or Wales'. The magpies entered the Barony of Forth, at Wexford's southeast tip and gradually spread throughout Ireland. This century's new Wexfordians include the emperor dragonfly: a splendid-looking creature of vibrant blue and bright green (that's the male; the female is all green). It arrived in 2000. Six years later, over 150 Essex skippers were seen at two locations. The appearance of this small, dark-edged, golden butterfly is puzzling, as it is not known to be a migrant. It may have arrived as eggs attached to hay brought in with horses. Skippers take their name from their swift, darting flight. They are on the wing now in south Wexford (and to a lesser extent, in Kildare). The wool-carder bee, which has a distinguishing line of yellow dots on either side of the abdomen, appeared in 2015. In 2017, the wasp orchid, a variant of the bee orchid

not recorded before, was found at Curracloe Beach by Paddy
Tobin, a retired schoolteacher and keen amateur.

16th 'a knife-thrower / hurling himself, a rainbow /
fractured...' Michael Longley's words can only
be about one creature: the magnificent kingfisher – as it
plunges towards its prey. Once seen, this surreal bird is never
forgotten; often it is just an electric streak of aquamarine and
turquoise shooting over a river or canal. The kingfisher, which
is a little larger and stockier than a robin, lives and breeds
on waterways and lakes all over Ireland, although it is less
prevalent in the west. The nest is in a long tunnel, burrowed
into an earthen bank. Often a pair will raise more than one
brood. Tidying up and grading of riverbanks can both destroy
existing nests and make the habitat inhospitable for future
attempts. Unpolluted water and a constant supply of fish
are essential, as it must eat its own weight in food each day.
The kingfisher hunts by sitting motionless on a perch, or
occasionally hovering over the water before diving to capture
small fish and aquatic insects. Although highly visible when
flying, when stationary it can merge into the background, its
rusty-orange breast melding with the multi-toned disorder of
waterside vegetation.

17th Take a mainline train journey or drive along
country roads, and you'll see scatters of creamy,
frothy meadowsweet in ditches and damp fields. Sometimes
it is accompanied by the upright green swords of yellow flag,
now finished flowering. Meadowsweet is indeed sweetly
scented: its summery perfume attracts insects, although its
flowers contain no nectar. They are rich in pollen, however,
and are often visited by crowds of tiny, shiny, black pollen
beetles. *Filipendula ulmaria* belongs to the rose family,
although it may not be immediately obvious. Look closely
and you'll see that the leaves are noticeably rose-like and

that the flower heads are similar to those of mountain ash or rowan, another member of the tribe. Meadowsweet was traditionally used as a painkiller; it contains salicylic acid, the ingredient in aspirin. An older botanical name was *Spiraea ulmaria*, which gives us the 'spir' in aspirin. The common name derives from the drink 'mead' (*meodu* in Old English), rather than 'meadow', as the plant was used to flavour mead, beer and other thirst quenchers. In Ireland, it was a remedy for dropsy, kidney trouble and sore throat.

18th At least two false widow spiders are frequent in Ireland, *Steatoda grossa* and *S. nobilis*, both natives of the Canary Islands. Their common name derives from the fact that they are of similar size and shape to the highly poisonous widow spiders – which do not occur here. The venom of false widows is not deadly, and the bites (rare, as these arachnids are sluggish and non-aggressive) are generally no worse than bee stings. Both *Steatoda* species are shiny, and appear hairless to the naked eye. Colouring ranges from black to reddish-brown and the abdomens are often marked in paler colours. In contrast to the beautifully woven, concentric webs of garden spiders, their webs are a chaotic mass of very strong strands. False widows live longer than our native spiders, and may pose a threat to local arachnids by outcompeting them. Researchers at the National University of Ireland in Galway have been studying the venom of *S. nobilis* for various properties, including its antimicrobial and anticancer possibilities.

19th Walk along any rocky seashore at low tide and you will find common limpets clinging to rocks with extraordinary tenacity. They are impossible to pull away. Yet, when the tide comes back in and these molluscs are again covered with water, they move about, grazing on the algae on the rock's surface. By the time the water has receded, each has returned to the exact same billet as before, a perfect and tight fit, abraded over time. Limpets have been known to live for seventeen years. Their radulae (mouthparts) are covered in tiny teeth. Research published in 2015 in the *Journal of the Royal Society Interface* claims that the teeth are made of the strongest-known material in nature – stronger than spider silk (the previous record-holder) and Kevlar, a manmade fibre. When feeding, limpets rasp away at the rock, which passes through their digestive tract and comes out the other end as tiny concrete blocks.

20th The pure white trumpet flowers of bindweed bring delight to non-gardeners, but to horticultural types, they indicate that the Battle of the Weeds has been lost. Blooming happens after the twining vines have crawled sneakily through flowerbeds, smothering shrubs and tying perennials together, to emerge triumphantly into a sunlit position. There are generally two bindweeds that invade gardens: hedge bindweed (*Calystegia sepium*), with flowers three to six centimetres across; and great bindweed (*C. silvatica*), up to eight centimetres across and with puffy, overlapping bracteoles – the modified leaves clasping the base of the trumpet. The latter species is sometimes considered a subspecies of the former. Although it may seem an unconscionable act of stupidity, *C. silvatica* was originally introduced as an ornamental garden plant. William Robinson (1838–1935), the great gardener and author, wrote: 'No plant forms more beautiful and delicate curtains of foliage and flowers than this, which grows vigorously in any soil.'

21st Flying ant season is upon us. Between now and the first part of August, virgin queens and males take to the air on a handful of warm, still days. They have been biding their time in the nest since hatching from their pupae. When the right weather conditions arise, all the new queens and males from a nest perform a nuptial flight, joining clouds of ants from other colonies. Millions fill the sky, bringing a food bonanza for gulls, starlings, swifts and other insect-eaters. Each queen flies speedily and evasively so that only the strongest males can catch up and mate with her. She copulates with several, storing their sperm in a spermatheca, a receptacle in her abdomen that can hold enough sperm to last for years. (Only female eggs are fertilised, so she doesn't have to use any to produce male offspring.) After mating, the males – their life's purpose completed – die. The queens shed their wings and crawl away to start their own nests, although very few succeed. Black garden ants (*Lasius niger*) are the most common species in urban and suburban areas. Queens can live a very long life: twenty-eight years is the greatest reported lifespan.

22nd Paths across dry or sandy soil are often perfumed with the warm, sweet and meadowy fragrance of lady's bedstraw – one of the classic scents of summer. The tiny, acid-yellow flowers of *Galium verum* make frothy eruptions on weak, straggling stems. The aroma lingers when the flowers are dried. They were used during mediaeval times to stuff mattresses in fine houses: hence 'my lady's bedstraw'. The new-mown-hay scent comes from coumarin, a chemical compound that has insecticidal properties, so the nose-pleasing plant also helped to repel fleas and other pests. According to European folklore, lady's bedstraw was in the manger at Bethlehem when Jesus was born. A vernacular name is 'cheese rennet' because the plant was used by cheesemakers to curdle milk. The flowers are visited by many flies and beetles, while several moths – including the magnificent hummingbird and elephant hawkmoths – lay their eggs on the plants. The related sweet woodruff (*G. odoratum*), which flowers in late spring in woodlands, also contains coumarin. Dried plants were once used as moth repellants and air fresheners. Both belong to *Rubiaceae*, the same family as cleavers or 'sticky backs'.

23rd Gardens and parks are full of adolescent birds. They are recognisable as members of their species, as their size and shape are right, but their plumage is still developing. Goldfinches are sporting black-and-yellow wings neatly chalked with white bars, but they lack the black-white-and-red masks of their parents. Blackbirds are brown, and are still wearing some of their infant, camouflaging speckles; immature blue tits look washed out and dull compared to the nattier grown-ups. Robins are getting the first flush of rusty red on their breasts. Young starlings have a patchy appearance: their flanks are clad in the white-spotted, dark feathers of adults, but the rest of their garb is still mouse-coloured. Their fights over choice scraps at bird feeders sound vicious, but watch a while and you'll see that mostly they are just standing and screaming into each other's faces. Few adult birds are singing now. Many are going through their moult and do not want to alert predators during this vulnerable period of shedding old, worn-out feathers and growing in fresh replacements.

24th The scarlet pimpernel is a tiny, missable annual plant that sprawls weakly on the surface of sandy soils, on waste ground and on the edges of cultivated places. *Anagallis arvensis*, in bloom from May until August, has five-petalled, orange-red flowers, not more than 1.5 centimetres across. Despite its diminutive size, this Irish native is the subject of much folklore. Those who carried it were supposed to be possessed of magical energies, including the abilities to understand the talk of animals and to trick others into false beliefs. Normally the flowers open in the morning and close again in mid-afternoon. However, the plant is sensitive to barometric pressure and folds over its petals when clouds or rain are on the way. This feature lends it vernacular names such as shepherd's clock and poor man's weather glass. In Irish, it is *seamair Mhuire*, Mary's shamrock – a name also given to common chickweed and common mouse-ear. A rare subspecies, *foemina* (once believed to be the female form), has blue flowers.

25th The so-called 'cabbage white' butterflies consist of two species: the large white (*Pieris brassicae*), with a wingspan of six to seven centimetres and pronounced black edges to the forewings; and the small white (*P. rapae*), a centimetre or two smaller and less clearly marked. Both are on the wing throughout the summer. Their caterpillars are hard at work now, munching voraciously on brassica plants such as kale, cabbage and turnip. The large white lays clusters of canary-coloured eggs that hatch into black-speckled, bile-yellow caterpillars. Its smaller relative lays single pale eggs that produce matte-green larvae. Brassicas are rich in sulphur-containing compounds – glucosinolates – which repel most pests. Not the white butterfly caterpillars, however, for their digestive system uses a special protein to counteract the toxins. Not only can they consume brassica leaves in bulk and with impunity, the toxins then act as the caterpillars' protectant, making them unpalatable to predators.

26th All too often, pretty flowers are less attractive to insects than they are to humans, but the ox-eye daisy is an all-round crowd-pleaser. For us, it is summer personified, as it brightens roadsides, meadows and other grassland with its dancing, egg-yolk-centred flowers. The fluttering, white ray florets of *Leucanthemum vulgare* are easy for insects to

spot from a distance, and they arrive in variety and quantity: bees, hoverflies, butterflies, tachinid flies, moths, beetles,
ants and wasps. They come for the pollen and nectar, but
often they stay to become lunch for a pale, camouflaged crab
spider crouching on the flower. At least half a dozen mi-
cro-moths (those with a wingspan under twenty millimetres)
lay their eggs on its foliage, which then feeds the caterpillars.
The plant was used in herbal medicine as a remedy for ab-
scesses and boils. One of its Irish names is *easpagán*: 'easpa'
translates as abscess, while 'easpag' means bishop. Through a
strange linguistic flip, bishop's posy is among its vernacular
names in Ulster.

27th Lavender is in season, carrying headily scented
batons of flower. Many plants sport blobs of white
spittle neatly attached to the stems. These are the nursery
places of the nymphs of the common froghopper insect
(*Philaenus spumarius*), one frothy globule per individual. The
immature bugs suck sap and repurpose it as a defensive foam,
masking them from predators and protecting them from heat,
cold and dehydration. They inhabit dozens of plants other than
lavender, but the spitballs are more obvious on its minimal
structure. Adult froghoppers vary in colour depending on
their surroundings, but are often grey or brownish. They are
champion high jumpers, able to spring seventy centimetres,
higher than a flea. Their greater body weight makes their
athleticism even more accomplished. The sudsy exudations
are also known as cuckoo spit, possibly because their first
appearance coincides with the arrival of the cuckoo. In recent
years, the little rosemary beetle (*Chrysolina americana*) has
started to appear on lavender – and others of its genus, including
sage and the eponymous rosemary. Despite its *americana*
handle, it is native to southern Europe, North Africa and parts
of Asia. Although it has pest status, it is a thing of beauty:
neatly striped in metallic wine-and-green.

28th If you're walking along a hedgerow on a summer evening and you spot a mouse, it's probably a wood mouse. Commonly known as the field mouse, it lives in a wide range of habitats, including grassland, woodland, sand dunes and raised bogs – almost anywhere it is not too wet. Wood mice are 'cuter' than house mice and have large, dark eyes and large, rounded ears. The fur is usually warmer and browner. If you get a glimpse of the belly – when one is shimmying up a stem, for example – you'll see it is pale. Wood mice arrived here during the Mesolithic Period, nine thousand years ago, about five thousand years before the house mouse. Their diet is wide-ranging: seeds, nuts, green plants, buds, fruits and fungi. In summer, at the height of the breeding season, insect larvae, worms and other invertebrates are consumed. Females give birth to more than one litter per season, with few of the young making it to the following year. They are an important item on the menu of many carnivores, including foxes and pine martens and raptors such as barn owls, red kites, kestrels and buzzards. When caught by the tail, a wood mouse can escape by shedding the tail's skin.

29th Common red soldier beetles are easy to spot now on flowers in meadows and hedgerows. The narrow, centimetre-long, orange or scarlet insects have black tips to their elytra (wing cases) and beady black eyes and antennae. The red-and-black combination gives rise to the 'soldier' epithet. They are obvious on yellow ragwort and on the white umbrellas of hogweed and angelica, and are often seen as mating pairs, which confers on them the delightful common name of bonking beetles. Copulation is leisurely for *Rhagonycha fulva*, often with the encumbered female rambling around on the flower head and both parties crunching pollen and sipping nectar during the act. These soft-bodied beetles are mainly carnivorous, however, and prey on smaller insects such as aphids. Eggs are laid near ground level, and the dark, velvety larvae feed on snails, slugs and other surface-dwelling invertebrates. The larvae hibernate, pupate in spring and emerge as adults in summer.

30th The oak is more than a tree. It is a world carpeted in lichens, mosses and liverworts, bristling with ferns, teeming with insects and visited by countless birds and mammals. A study published by the Environmental Information Data Centre in the UK found 2,300 species associated with the oak. (We have a smaller pool of species in Ireland, but if only half that amount is oak-connected, it would still be impressive.) Oaks have been part of our heritage for thousands of years: the timber was employed in shipbuilding, construction and furniture, the bark and acorns were used for tanning leather and dyeing fabric, and whole forests were burned while smelting iron ore. The Irish for oak is *dair*, while an oakwood is *doire*, words that give us the placenames of Kildare, Edenderry and Derry. In recent centuries most oak woods have been planted by humans, but in earlier times, the jay was responsible for propagating the trees. The birds cache acorns for later use. Those that they press into the ground are sometimes forgotten and grow into saplings.

31st A handful of hawk-moths are found in Ireland. Only one, the hummingbird hawk-moth, is a daytime flyer, so it is seen most often. *Macroglossum stellatarum* is remarkably bird-like, with a feathery body and wings, a bunch of bristles that form a tail, and dark points – pseudopupils – in the eyes. It hovers while drinking nectar, and its lengthy proboscis can be seen flexed like a whip (*macroglossum* means 'long tongue'). The orange-and-brown moth migrates from the southern Mediterranean and North Africa; the greatest numbers are seen in June and July. Buddleja, red valerian and lavender are favoured plants.

A relative that appears here occasionally is the death's-head hawk-moth (*Acherontia atropos*), made famous by the film, *The Silence of the Lambs*. The thorax carries the markings of a skull and the wingspan is up to 135 millimetres, making it the largest moth found in Ireland.

August

1st Teasel is in flower on roadsides and waste ground and in the gardens of nature lovers. The prehistoric-looking, spiny plant is unmistakable thanks to its statuesque height of two to three metres, and its angular stems and bristling flower heads. Its lilac florets appear in neat bands around its prickly, egg-shaped finials. They are much visited by bees, hoverflies and butterflies. The leaf axils – where stem and leaves join – form receptacles, known as phytotelmata, that catch rainwater. It is possible that these pools prevent ants and other crawling insects (inefficient pollinators of such tall species) reaching the flowers. Hapless invertebrates drown in the cups, nutrifying the water which then becomes a tiny ecosystem supporting countless microscopic creatures and various algae. In autumn, *Dipsacus fullonum* dries to make a fine, upstanding skeleton, and goldfinches appear to winkle the seeds from the plant's hedgehog-like heads. Dried teasel heads were once used to brush the surface of woven fabrics, as part of the finishing or 'fulling' process – a word that is reflected in the Latin name.

2nd Dive-bombing and aggressive 'seagulls' are in the news every summer. The offenders are herring gulls – originally coastal residents breeding on rocky outcrops and feeding on fish and other foods in the intertidal area. They are naturally opportunistic and have long come inland to follow the plough, taking worms and other invertebrates uncovered by the blades. More recently, loss of habitat and declining fish stocks have forced them to forage among the leftovers discarded by humans in dumps and in urban areas.

Herring gulls are huge and handsome birds with silver-grey wings and back, black-and-white-edged wing tips and a yellow bill marked with a blood-red spot. Juveniles are flecked with grey and brown, and do not fully develop adult plumage until four years old. Folklore says that when gulls come inland, bad weather is on the way. However, on warm summer days they are often seen wheeling acrobatically over the land, hawking for flying ants. Herring gulls can live for over thirty years.

3rd Visitors to the west and southwest delight in the fringes of cheerful orange montbretia decorating ditches and roadsides. Although it is luxuriantly at home in the wilds of Ireland, *Crocosmia* x *crocosmiiflora* is neither wild nor Irish. It is a hybrid of two South African species, *Crocosmia aurea* and *C. pottsii*, and was bred in France by the prolific Lemoine nursery. The plant was introduced to gardens in 1879, where its profusion of petite flame-coloured trumpets and sword-shaped leaves were an instant success. Its rapidly multiplying corms meant that it soon became too much of a good thing and gardeners tossed it over cliffs and into dumps and ditches. A single errant corm, no larger than an acorn, is sufficient to start a new colony. Montbretia is present throughout Ireland: it particularly enjoys the mild and moist conditions of counties Kerry and Cork, where it overwhelms the native flora.

4th If you find neat circles and ovals in the leaves of your rose bushes, congratulate yourself, for leafcutter bees have been at work. We have five species of *Megachile* solitary bees. They look roughly similar to honeybees, but the females gather pollen under their abdomens, instead of in 'pollen baskets' on the legs. All are cavity nesters, and those that frequent gardens use holes in masonry or wood, hollow plant stems and even items such as disused hose pipes. The female slices out pieces of leaf (and sometimes petals) to line the walls of the nest chamber. She lays a single egg and adds a ball of pollen and nectar to feed the larva. After sealing the chamber with leaf discs, she lines the next section of the tunnel with oval pieces, lays another egg, and so on. When the larvae hatch, they consume their food parcels, settle down to pupate and emerge as adults some months later. Dozens of plants besides roses may be clipped for nest material. Among them are silver birch, cherry, fuchsia, rosebay willowherb and wild strawberry.

5th Go for a walk on a country lane or on waste ground now, and you are likely to encounter lesser burdock. *Arctium minus* is an upright plant with great felted leaves, once used for wrapping butter. The pinky-purple, thistle-like flowers develop into bristly seedheads covered in hooked burrs, which attach readily to clothes or animal fur. The hitch-hiking seeds are thus dispersed at some distance from the parent plant. In 1941, the burrs provided inspiration to Swiss engineer George de Mestral for his invention, the hook-and-loop fastener, Velcro. They are also celebrated in the Burry Man festival in South Queensferry, near Edinburgh, which dates back to at least 1687. This takes place on the second Friday in August when a man, wearing head-to-toe flannel underwear and balaclava, is covered in burrs so that his entire body is encased in prickles. Thus attired he processes through the town for the whole day, led by a bell-ringing boy and followed by strings of supporters. In Irish folk remedies, burdock was used to cure an impressive range of ailments including: a bad stomach, burns, cough, kidney trouble, skin disease, scurvy, yellow jaundice, sores, nettle stings, fits, convulsions and 'weak blood'.

6th Holly blues that hatched from eggs laid in spring on their namesake plant have been on the wing for a week or two in some places. These tiny butterflies are an ethereal,

Virgin-Mary blue, and they dance lightly through the air, stopping occasionally at flowers to take nectar. This generation will lay their eggs mainly on ivy, but some will choose alder, bramble, raspberry, dogwood, willow, gorse and other plants. There are also great numbers of small white and large white butterflies flying about. At times the last two species can be difficult to distinguish from each other, as the dimensions of each are not uniform, and there is some overlap in size. The former usually has black markings extending farther down the outer edges of the forewings than the latter. In gardens, both habitually lay their eggs on members of the cabbage family. They often choose nasturtiums also.

7th Hemp agrimony, a stately, native perennial of up to two metres, is in flower along ditches and in marshes, wet woodlands and other damp places. Its upright stems are topped with tight clusters of dusty pink blooms. A hundred florets are crammed into each square centimetre of the inflorescence, with the pale, protruding stigmas creating a layer of fuzz. *Eupatorium cannabinum* is a popular late-summer forage plant for many flying insects, including over twenty butterfly species. Both the common and botanical names refer to the leaves, which at a distance look like those of cannabis or hemp. This confusion has led to one of its vernacular names, reported from Donegal and parts of Britain: 'holy rope'. It was mistakenly believed to have supplied the hempen fibres that made the ropes with which Jesus Christ was bound. In Irish, it is *cnáib uisce* (water hemp) or *sceachóg Mhuire* – Mary's little bush. Although the resemblance is not easy to spot, it is a member of the daisy family.

8th Fruit fly season is upon us in our kitchens and fruit bowls. These small insects with their lazy, drifting movements and malevolent-looking red eyes are more correctly known as vinegar flies. They are attracted to the yeasts and bacteria that grow on overripe or damaged fruit. Thirty species of *Drosophila* have been recorded in Ireland. The best-known is the so-called common fruit fly (*D. melanogaster*), which has been used in laboratory experiments for over a century. About 75 per cent of human disease-causing genes are shared with the species. Its short life cycle (seven to ten days from egg to adult in a warm habitat) and other factors make it an ideal model for studying human diseases and other stressors. The fruit fly was the first creature to be sent into space, in 1947. Thousands are regularly sent up in the International Space Station. Indeed, as you are reading this, a crowd of them may well be orbiting the earth.

9th Manx shearwaters are here now to breed. The greatest colonies are found in County Kerry, especially in the Blasket Islands. Along the east coast, there are sizeable colonies on the Saltee Islands off County Wexford, and on County Down's Copeland Island. In autumn, they will head down to the south Atlantic off South America. They will not return to land again until the breeding season. 'Manxies' are black on top and white underneath and have enormously long wings. They have a low and fast flight that, true to their name, shears the water. Rapid wingbeats are followed by long aircraft-like glides, often tilting, with the bird alternately flashing white and black. Shearwaters are clumsy on the ground, crawling awkwardly to their nest burrows, and landing only on dark nights to avoid being predated by gulls. The birds are mute when at sea, but on land they call constantly with strange cackling, coughing and wheezing notes. Although its Latin name is *Puffinus puffinus*, the Manx shearwater is not related to the puffin. The species is remarkably long-lived, with the oldest known bird estimated to be fifty-five years or older. It was ringed on Copeland Island in 1953 when approximately five years old, and was caught again and released in 2003.

10th One of our most common hoverflies is the marmalade fly, which has a somewhat flattened body. Its clear and distinctive gold-and-black pattern is not difficult to recognise: the individual stripes are variously narrow and broad, while the two amber bands nearest the thorax are broken in the middle. The dull green or brown larvae of *Episyrphus balteatus* are aphidophagous, meaning that they are aphid-eaters, while the adults feed on both pollen and nectar. If you grow lilies or other plants with prominent anthers, marmalade flies will appear, holding the stamens with their front legs while they gather the pollen. The species is migratory, and local populations can be augmented by massive swarms arriving from Europe in late summer. They, in turn, are following clouds of aphids. Many hoverflies are tricky to identify to species level, but it is usually easy to distinguish the sexes. Males have large eyes that meet along the top of the head. The eyes of females are smaller and set farther apart. When mating, the male often places his front legs in the gap between the female's eyes.

11th August and September may seem unlikely months for songbirds to nest, but several species, including blackbird, goldfinch, greenfinch, spotted flycatcher, willow warbler, stonechat and yellowhammer, may still be home-building and raising chicks. Some of these are on their second or third brood. Others, however, such as the yellowhammer and the spotted flycatcher, are late starters and may still be looking after their first lot of chicks, or just beginning to care for their second. Both are vulnerable species (the first is red-listed, while the second is amber). Changes in agriculture, falling invertebrate numbers and habitat destruction have all played a part in putting these birds at risk. Yellowhammers are pretty yellow-and-brown birds, slightly larger and more elongated than a sparrow. Males have vibrant yellow heads and breasts in the breeding season and sing cheerfully all day: 'a-little-bit-of-bread-and-no-cheeeeese'. They once bred all over Ireland, but are now restricted to the east and south. The adults feed on grains, and the lack of cereal fields has led to a decrease in numbers. Hedgecutting during the coming weeks can wreak havoc with breeding birds, not just those that build their nests in hedgerows, but those that are feeding insects to their young.

12th Rock samphire has been in flower all summer along our coasts. This is such a pleasing-looking plant, with its pale grey-green foliage neatly divided into twos and its lacy, ivory flower heads. A healthy specimen is so regular and nicely proportioned that it might be the design for a Liberty fabric or a William Morris wallpaper. *Crithmum maritimum* is a member of the carrot family. It grows on shingle, among rocks and on stony cliffs, and is also known as sea samphire or sea fennel. In French, it is 'herbe de Saint Pierre': the contraction of 'Saint Pierre' gives us the English 'samphire'. At one time it was regularly collected for food, and in Ireland was eaten raw, boiled or pickled. Those who collected it often gathered it from steep rock faces, a perilous job. It is mentioned in *King Lear* when Edgar and Gloucester are looking over the dizzying cliffs of Dover: 'half way down / Hangs one that gathers samphire, dreadful trade!' The samphire of restaurants and food markets (*Salicornia*) is an unrelated plant that grows in salt marshes. It is also known as glasswort as its ashes (containing significant quantities of sodium) were once used in the making of glass.

13th One day the sky is full of swifts, gliding and swooping while hunting for insects or screaming past in supercharged squadrons of twenty or more birds. The next, they are gone, winging their way back to central and southern Africa. They spend three months or less here, arriving in late April or early May and leaving mostly between mid-July and now. During that brief period, pairs raise one or two chicks in roof crevices and holes in buildings. They line the nest with feathers, hairs and shreds of grass that they catch in the air and bind together with saliva. If insects are scarce, parents may travel great distances (even to Wales) in search of supplies. During lean periods, chicks enter a torpid state which can last for up to ten days, conserving energy by lowering body temperature and slowing the heart rate. Swifts' shrill cries, inky silhouettes and frenzied aerobatics have earned them the name of 'devil birds'. Yet, these dark angels of the air are in trouble: modern roofs are carefully sealed, denying them access. Nest boxes can be retrofitted, while new-builds can incorporate nest bricks. Swift nests are tidy, zero-waste affairs: chicks produce faecal sacs, which the adults remove. During the first weeks after hatching, the parents often consume the sacs, thus recycling the nutrients.

14th Honeysuckle, also known as woodbine, twines through our hedgerows all year, but its presence is obvious only during summer when its sweetly-scented, pink-tinged yellow flowers appear. They are tubular and flare-topped, with prominent stamens and stigma, and are unlike those of any other native plant. The lengthy tube means that the nectar can be reached only by long-tongued insects such as the garden bumblebee and certain moths. The flowers of *Lonicera periclymenum* are followed by bright red berries. *Féithleann* was widely used in Irish folk remedies to bathe sore eyes and ears and as a potion to combat jaundice – although the foul taste of the cure was considered worse than the jaundice itself. A riddle from Limerick collected as part of a nationwide schools project in the 1930s goes like so: Why is the letter A like a honeysuckle? Because it is followed by a B.

15th We have several willowherbs. Most commonly seen, but often not noticed except by picky gardeners, is the tiny broad-leaved willowherb (*Epilobium montanum*), a skinny plant with pale pink flowers that stealthily appears in flower beds. More obvious is the tall, magenta-spired rosebay willowherb (*Chamaenerion angustifolium*), which makes colonies of dozens (and eventually hundreds) of plants, often on roadsides or banks. Its fluffy, parachuted seed is floating on the breeze now. The great willowherb (*Epilobium hirsutum*) has fewer blooms per plant, but they are conspicuous for their distinctive, creamy, cross-shaped stigmas, which give the rose-toned flowers an ornamental quality. A rarer all-white form exists. Great willowherb is the larval food plant for several moths, including the magnificently cartoonish caterpillars of the elephant hawk-moth. These mud-coloured, finger-sized larvae have clownish pseudo-eyes to scare off predators. The adult moths fly at night and are beautiful pink-and-olive creatures.

16th This month is still good for butterfly spotting, especially in wild places with plenty of flowering plants – including woodland edges, hedgerows and grasslands. Among the best sites are limestone areas such as the Burren, and coastal dune systems such as at the Raven Nature Reserve in County Wexford. The two largest of our four fritillaries are on the wing now. The silver-washed and dark-green are showy butterflies with delicate inky dots and squiggles on a rust background. The smaller pearl-bordered fritillary is confined to Galway and Clare: the adults are gone and only the caterpillars remain, hiding in leaf litter and emerging to graze and sunbathe. The marsh fritillary, another small butterfly (42–47 millimetre wingspan), is a protected species. Chequered with a glowing mosaic of orange and yellow on warm brown, the Irish form is more brightly marked than its British counterpart. You won't see adult butterflies now, but you may see the remarkable larval webs among devil's-bit scabious, the food plant. The black, fuzzy caterpillars work communally to spin protective sheets of silk, which may shelter over a hundred individuals. They pupate in late spring and will begin to hatch as adults in May.

17th Poppy seedheads are the salt-shakers of the plant world. After the petals fall, the capsule swells and dries and a series of apertures open underneath the brim. When the wind rocks the stem, the seeds are dispensed at a distance from the plant. If dug into the soil by the activities of nature, man or animal, seeds can lie dormant but viable for decades. Disturbing the ground triggers them into germination, as happened in the fields around Ypres and the Somme when red poppies appeared after the carnage of the First World War. *Papaver rhoeas* has been an agricultural weed for so long that its native region is unknown. Its seeds were found mixed in with barley in Egyptian artefacts dating from before 2500 BCE. In Irish folk medicine *cailleach dearg* was believed to have narcotic properties (probably because of a confusion with its relative, the opium poppy), and was recommended for toothache, headache, mumps and for restless babies.

18th We are entering the wandering wasp season. Redundant workers start roaming around and getting into drinks, sweet foods and overripe fruits. Until now, they have been members of a highly organised army of builders, cleaners, foragers, hunters and nurses, all billeted in a thousands-strong nest. But nests have a lifespan of just a few months: the reigning queens toil themselves to death through establishing colonies and intensively laying eggs. As they fade, the nest falls apart and cannibalism sets in. New queens emerge to mate with the males (a batch of which has been raised solely for this purpose), often with multiple partners. The males die and some of the queens will hibernate and start new colonies in spring. The sterile workers, meanwhile, have neither jobs nor a ready source of food. Previously, they had fed on sugary secretions from the larvae, and they are now in search of alternative sustenance. They will die soon. Wasps get bad press at this time of the year, but while the nest is active, they collect vast quantities of aphids, larvae and other slow-moving (that is, plant-munching) invertebrates. So, they are allies of gardeners.

19th Country roadsides are decorated with occasional flutters of pale pink flowers on knee- or thigh-high plants. They look conspicuous among our native flora, as if a bit of cottage garden has jumped the hedge. Indeed, this is often what has happened: soapwort is an introduced species, grown at one time for use as a natural cleanser for clothing and wool. Some of the clumps we see were discarded from gardens, others mark where cottages or other buildings once stood. Almost all Irish plants are a double-flowered form, where the stamens are replaced by extra petals. They are infertile and produce no seeds, and are able to reproduce only by fragments taking root. *Saponaria officinalis* had many uses, including as a cleaning agent for fragile fabrics such as silks, antique curtains and tapestries. Both the National Trust and the Victoria and Albert Museum have employed it. Caleb Threlkeld notes that a decoction of soapwort, bladder campion and '*Scordonia*' (which may be either garlic or wood sage) 'are effectual against the *Lues venerea* [syphilis] according to some good Authors'. Don't try this at home.

20th Birds raising their voices during this last month are not very tuneful. We have been listening to the raucous clatters and caws from magpies and other corvids, the chattering of starlings and sparrows, and the screeches and babylike wails of gulls. Perhaps the prettiest are the repetitive 'coo-COO-coo' of the collared doves and those of the wood pigeons (who manage an extra two coos per phrase). Occasionally, there are fly-bys of goldfinches with their tinkling calls. Many birds have been raising their young and moulting – a time for being secretive and quiet, not calling attention to yourself. Robins are among the first to start singing again and establishing their domains. Unusually, males and females carve out separate territories for winter, so there is more competition among this species than others. In the coming weeks, they will be singing and scolding more frequently as they bicker over boundaries.

21st Clear days with calm seas are the best for spotting whales and other cetaceans. So, if the weather is fine, head for a headland or cliff (but mind your step) and scan the water with binoculars or telescope. Look for sea bird activity, as predators such as whales and dolphins chase fish up to the surface, and birds – including gannets, auks and shearwaters – gather to take part in the feeding. Over twenty-five cetacean species have been spotted in Irish waters, but those that we are most likely to see from land include harbour porpoises; bottlenose and Risso's dolphins; and minke and humpback whales. The larger mammals are almost exclusively seen off the Atlantic and south coasts, where marine life is more abundant and diverse. The edges of Kerry and Cork offer the best chances of sightings. Sadly, the over-fished Irish Sea provides poor sustenance for these magnificent creatures. The Shannon Estuary is home to a population of well over a hundred bottle-nosed dolphins. Ireland's most famous member of that species is Fungie, a wild dolphin who has interacted with humans for the last thirty years in Dingle, County Kerry.

22nd The bramble berry is a vexing berry, not just because it sets painful booby traps with its great looping, thorny stems, but because it is a taxonomic nightmare. Rather than being one simple species, *Rubus fructicosus* is an aggregate of many microspecies. Hundreds have been identified, and at least 100 of them exist in Ireland. The differences are often so minute that they can be discerned only by expert botanists. Most years the fruits are beginning to turn black and juicy around now. Blackbirds, thrushes and robins are among the first wave of birds to eat them, while later, flocks of raucous starlings will descend to feed. The bird receives a nutritious meal, and in return acts as a dispersal mechanism, depositing the undigested seed at some distance from the parent plant. However, some birds – bullfinches and blue tits, for example – are 'seed predators', cracking open the seeds and rendering them useless for spreading the plant's progeny. Bramble thickets also give birds a safe place to nest and roost. The species is one of the larval food plants for holly blue and green hairstreak butterflies and for many moths.

23rd Lizards make their home in Ireland, even though our misty, damp climate may not seem hospitable. The viviparous or common lizard is native to a wide range of habitats, including grassland, woodland, bog, mountain sides and coastal sites. The little reptile needs a warm basking spot (rocks, sand or dry timber) with nearby shelter into which it can sprint for cover. *Zootoca vivipara* is present in a broad band across Europe and Asia, from the west of Ireland to the Pacific coast of Japan. In warmer areas, such as the Mediterranean, the lizard lays eggs, but in colder regions such as here, the eggs are retained within the female's body. After hatching, the miniature baby lizards (numbering three to twelve) are 'born'. Young lizards are around now, as are gravid females, basking to keep the eggs warm in their swollen bellies. In winter viviparous lizards 'brumate' (a process similar to hibernation) and may emerge on mild days. Occasionally one sees a lizard lacking a tail (or, indeed, the tail without the lizard). In emergencies, they are able to shed their tails, a process that may confuse predators, and save lizard lives.

24th The most striking native plant along our roadsides at present is purple loosestrife, a handsome, upright perennial (1–2 metres high), with vibrant magenta spires of flower. The plants are not consistent, and flowers may have five or six petals, and varying formats of stamens and styles. *Lythrum salicaria* favours damp hedgerows, ditches, marshes and water sides. Native to Europe and Asia, the wild plant is showy enough to be included in some of Ireland's finest gardens. It is less welcome in north America, where it has become aggressively invasive. It was introduced there over two centuries ago, possibly in ships' ballast, or as a medicinal or ornamental plant. The first records in the wild date from 1814, when it was observed in wet meadows in Canada and New England. Purple loosestrife is now present in forty-eight states, where massive colonies choke wetlands, crowding out native species and harming biodiversity. In Ireland it is fed upon by the caterpillars of the powdered quaker moth and the small elephant hawk-moth.

25th Those who keep poultry are familiar with the sight of hens indulging in a communal dust bath. Among garden birds, however, such convivial grooming is rare. Sparrows are an exception, and given a patch of dry soil, groups of ten or twenty will flutter and tumble about, thoroughly coating their feathers. The dust acts like a dry shampoo for plumage, mopping up excess oil and loosening dry skin and other matter. It may also help to dislodge or smother lice and mites. After a good shake, the sparrow rearranges its feathers and coats them with oil from the preen gland, which sits above the base of the tail. The waxy oil helps weatherproof the feathers; it also has antimicrobial and antifungal properties that act as a defence against disease and parasites. Research suggests that the preen oil in healthy male sparrows has cosmetic properties that affect badge size – the black throat patch that signifies status.

26th Ash trees are laden with dense clusters of seeds, hanging palely from the branches like huge bunches of keys (another name for them). When they ripen, they will be eaten by birds and small mammals. Dozens of insects are dependent on the tree, including the centre-barred sallow and coronet moths. Both are on the wing now and laying eggs on it, as well as on privet (which belongs to the same family, *Oleaceae*, the olive family). Carry a bunch of ash keys, and you will be protected against witchcraft. In Norse mythology, Yggdrasil was the ash tree at the centre of the cosmos. Shakespeare's Roman general Coriolanus was so strong and fearsome that he continually shattered the lance of his rival, Aufidius: the 'grained ash an hundred times hath broke, / And scarr'd the moon with splinters.' Normally, the wood is robust, flexible and shock absorbent, which makes it perfect for hurleys.

27th A joke: 'What's worse than finding a worm in the apple you just took a bite of?' Answer: 'Finding half a worm.' (And, one might add, a dark glob of frass or insect excrement.) Most often the culprit – or half culprit – is the larva of the codling moth. Adults are insignificant-looking brown insects with a wingspan of about seventeen millimetres. When at rest, the wings, which have a dull gold splotch on the edges, fold into a tent-like shape. Mated females are attracted to the scent of fermentation from ripening fruits, and often lay their eggs on them or nearby. The odour indicates the presence of fermenting sugars and microbes, which are nourishing food for larvae and adults alike. The Latin name for the species is *Cydia pomonella*. A popular 'jailbreaking' software for bypassing the Apple iOS system was named Cydia by its creator, American software engineer Jay Freeman, in honour of the 'worm in the apple'.

28th The last of our orchids to bloom is the dainty autumn lady's tresses, which has tubular white flowers spiralling around the stem – an arrangement that gives us the Latin name, *Spiranthes spiralis*. They are pollinated by bumblebees, which usually start at the base and corkscrew their way up to the top of the inflorescence. The slender stems are often no taller than fifteen centimetres. Lie flat on your stomach, look through a hand lens and you'll see that if you were being fanciful, the winding flower buds could resemble a tiny braid of hair. *Cúilín Muire* (meaning 'Mary's hair' – specifically, the hair on the back of the head) grows on nutrient-poor ground such as dry turf, older dunes and limestone pavement. The largest concentrations are found in the far west (Galway, Clare and the Cork peninsulas) and in the 'sunny southeast' of Wexford and Waterford. The leaves of *Spiranthes spiralis* wither before the flower spikes emerge, making it doubly difficult to spot, but there is always a little rosette of leaves to one side – the locus for next year's flowers. New plants develop a root system underground for up to eleven years before the first leaf emerges.

29th The magpie is not an easy bird to love in spring and summer when it is raiding other birds' nests for eggs and even nestlings. But now that the main nesting season is over, it returns to a diet of insects, berries and all manner of food scraps. The coming months offer plenty of opportunities for magpie admiration, as the birds are present in over 90 per cent of Irish gardens. While their plumage may look black-and-white from a distance, when close up, its full magnificence is revealed. The wings and tail are an iridescent mix of deep blues and greens. Magpies, along with other corvids, were reputed to bring misfortune. According to folklore collected in County Leitrim, the magpie is a 'very unlucky bird because she is a crossbred between a raven and a dove' and was the only bird who did not go in mourning when Christ was crucified.

30th The reddish-brown seedheads of dock are standing tall and proud in fields and on roadsides. Against the buff-tipped, end-of-summer grass they stand out starkly – as if drawn with sepia ink. Our most common species is broad-leaved dock (*Rumex obtusifolius*), with its rosette of coarse foliage. For centuries the leaves have been used as a remedy for nettle stings, although their effect may be merely that the sap helps cool the irritation. Nettles and dock often grow in similar environments, and the search for the curative leaf may provide a distraction that alleviates the discomfort. Dock seeds have great longevity, and can germinate after sixty years when turned over in the soil. At the end of the Second World War, dock was one of the more common of the 126 plant species recorded on bomb sites by Professor Edward Salisbury, director of the Royal Botanic Gardens at Kew.

31st The clusters of berries on mountain ash (also known as rowan) are turning red now. Many of our street trees are special cultivated varieties, with more upright and more oval heads than that of the native mountain ash, *Sorbus aucuparia*. In the wild the tree grows by mountain streams and in glens and rocky places, where it is a lovely sight. It is frequently seen in hedgerows, where it may have been planted. The fruits are eagerly eaten by blackbirds, thrushes, blackcaps and bullfinches, among others. The specific epithet, *aucuparia*, comes from the Latin *aucupor*, to go bird-catching. Occasionally a mistle thrush will take possession of a single tree and fight off all other birds. In winter, if times are hard in northern Europe, flocks of beautiful and debonair waxwings may arrive to feed. These elegant birds, which are a little smaller than starlings, have sleek, beige-grey plumage with black and white accents on face and wings. A patch of intensely red feathers on each wing resembles a drop of sealing wax – which gives rise to the name. Waxwings often descend upon suburban areas where the trees have been planted in quantity.

September

1^{**st**} The season of fabulous webs is upon us. After the cooler nights, the silken creations of orb weavers such as the brown-and-cream garden spider (*Araneus diadematus*) are shimmeringly outlined in morning dew. Webs are composed of two kinds of silk, which serve different purposes. The radial threads (the spokes) absorb and dissipate the kinetic energy of insects that fly into the web, preventing them from trampolining back to freedom. The spiral threads, meanwhile, adhere to the prey, giving the spider time to reach it and subdue it. The gluey fibres are very extensible, but have little elastic force, so the prey has nothing to push against to free itself. Webs are rebuilt regularly, and the protein-rich silk is consumed and recycled. Male garden spiders, which are smaller and slimmer than the pea-sized females, go in search of mates in autumn. The male approaches the female carefully, as a hasty suitor can easily become supper. After mating, the female retreats to a sheltered place and spins a receptacle for her 100–800 eggs. She dies shortly after filling and sealing the egg sac. The spiderlings – yellow with a black mark on the abdomen – hatch in spring. It will be another eighteen months before they are ready to mate.

2^{**nd**} While many wildflowers are deep into the business of shedding and spreading seed now, a few are still in peak flowering mode. Among them are the woundworts. There are a handful of species, but the most common and noticeable are the hedge and marsh woundworts (*Stachys sylvatica* and *S. palustris*), which can reach close to a metre in height. Both have a strong, upright stance and square stems bearing robust spires of flowers in dusty maroon and pinkish-violet, respectively. Those of the latter are as beautifully marked with nectar guides as an orchid. The common name comes from their traditional use in healing wounds, and indeed, modern experiments have revealed antiseptic properties. Hedge woundwort is also known as staggerweed, as livestock that eat too many of the seedheads can be afflicted with staggering, shivering and other nerve-related disorders. Woundworts belong to the same genus that includes the endearingly furry garden plant, lamb's ears (*S. byzantina*).

3rd Small copper butterflies are out and about. Although a bright insect, with black-spotted, tangerine-toned forewings, it can be difficult to spot. It is a fast mover and is tiny, with a wingspan of just 26–36 millimetres. When the wings are folded, it becomes a paper-thin, grey-brown shard, with barely-there slivers of orange. Numbers swell in early summer and again around now, as each generation reaches maturity. The species overwinters in caterpillar form – a small green blob attached to a leaf or stem with a pad of silk. Food plants are common and sheep sorrel and broad-leaved dock. In warm years, instead of bedding down for the cold months, the caterpillar offspring of the late-summer generation complete their life cycle and emerge in autumn. They are sometimes on the wing in late October and even into November. Adults that are around now may be the second or third generation this year. A distinctive race exists in Ireland, *Lycaena phlaeas* subsp. *hibernica*; its variations include a broader colour band on the hindwing.

4th The hips on roses are ripening. Most fall into the narrow colour band between deep wine and terracotta orange. However, those of the little burnet rose (*Rosa pimpinellifolia*) are like the shiny black beads on a large, heavy-duty rosary. This ground-hugging plant grows in the

Burren, as well as in sandy, coastal regions. It is the first of the wild roses to flower, in May and June, when it produces small, sweetly scented blooms of white, cream or palest pink. Another inhabitant of seaside areas is the rugose rose (*R. rugosa*) from northeast Asia. It is planted for its tolerance to salt and wind, but it often takes off on a mission of its own, colonising by suckering shoots. Birds eat the rotund, fleshy hips and help to spread the seed about. Fruits of the dog rose (*R. canina*) and its hybrids (it crosses with several other roses) are also foraged by birds. According to folklore collected in the 1930s, rosehips were gathered by children and threaded onto wire or strings to make necklaces, bracelets and headbands.

5th It's such a joy to come across a froglet, no bigger than your little finger nail, but perfect in all its frogginess. These tiny creatures have beaten the odds: thousands of eggs are laid by each female, but those that make it past the tadpole stage are few and far between. This year's freshly minted froglings still have countless hurdles to hop. Many will meet their ends in the clamping bills of ducks, herons, gulls and other predators. Those that survive into their third year and become sexually mature may be in single figures. The common frog (*Rana temporaria*) is not so common any more: modern agriculture and development have wiped out many habitats. Garden ponds, parks and other manmade bodies of water are crucial territories now. In times past, frogs were used in various folk cures. A remedy collected from County Waterford in the 1930s goes like this: 'It is said that if you had a toothache and you put a frog into your mouth and left him there until he "screeched" three times you would be cured immediately.'

6th Walk along a bit of dry waste ground, or inspect the cracks of paving where weedkiller is not used, and you may see rosettes of large grey-green leaves with a soft, felted texture. These are the distinctive seedlings of the native great mullein (*Verbascum thapsus*), whose natural habitat is gravelly banks and sandy soils. It is a biennial plant, and next summer it will send up a single knobbly broom-handle of yellow flowers. In Irish, it is *coinnle Mhuire* – Mary's candle – because it suggests a tall, lighted taper. Among the many vernacular names are flannelwort, hag taper, Aaron's rod and poor man's blanket. This year's tall plants are almost spent, but after dying the dried spires will persist staunchly throughout winter, providing seeds for birds such as blue tits, red polls and goldfinches, as well as a roosting place for invertebrates such as earwigs. It is said that the Ancient Romans used to dip the dried stalks in tallow and use them as candles.

7th The stems of some plants are scattered with crowds of matte black insects. These are black bean aphids, *Aphis fabae*. They take their name from the broad bean (*Vicia faba*), but they live on many plants besides beans, including teasel, artichoke, nasturtium and dock. In each little gathering, a few individuals have wings: these are the migrants that will fly off to other plants and start new settlements. Soon they will move to their last quarters of the year, on spindle, viburnum and philadelphus (mock orange), where they will mate and lay eggs, which hatch next spring. It's worth examining an aphid congregation under magnification, especially if you want to introduce a child to the weirdness of nature. Look for ants moving among them and gathering honeydew, the waste plant sap that aphids excrete. The ants busily pat and stroke the aphids until – magic! – they produce a clear bubble of liquid from their rear end. The relationship is mutual, as ants protect their 'herds' from predators, chasing away ladybird larvae and other aphid eaters.

8th Gardens are like busy train stations this month. Birds pass through on their way in and out of Ireland, and flocks of young adults are on the move, crowding around feeders and food plants like teenagers at vending machines. Willow warblers and chiffchaffs are among the passers-through – dainty little birds, just larger than a wren. They forage skittishly at ground level and amid foliage, searching for invertebrates. The two species are famously difficult to differentiate. Both are pale, sandy-olive birds, lighter underneath and greeny-grey on top. Chiffchaffs usually have near-black legs, while those of willow warblers are paler and pinker, and the plumage is often brighter. Experienced birders do a quick scan of these characteristics, as well as the wing feathers: those of willow warblers are longer. Song is the defining feature: willow warblers are more mellifluous than their onomatopoeic relative with its repetitive 'chiff-chaff ... chiff-chaff'. At this time of the year, however, both are calling rather than singing, and both, confusingly, with a variation of 'hoo-eet'. The willow warbler's voice is a little less reedy than that of the chiffchaff, but it is still difficult to be sure. Those of us who are still uncertain about an ID settle for 'willow-chiffs'.

9th The speckled wood is one of our most frequently recorded butterflies, found in dappled shade in woodlands, hedgerows and gardens. Its distinctive brown wings with their highly contrasting cream spots make it easy to identify. Additionally, each forewing has a black-and-white eye-spot on the upper edge, while hindwings have three at the base. There are two or three broods per year, so individuals can be seen on the wing almost continuously from late spring to autumn. They are adaptable insects and can overwinter either in caterpillar or chrysalis form. Adults rarely visit flowers to take nectar; instead they mop up honeydew (the sugar-rich secretions of aphids) from leaves. Males defend their few square metres of territory aggressively. The incumbent skirmishes with trespassers, with the two butterflies whirling around in a spiralling double helix until the interloper flees. Speckled woods are approximately the same size as the small tortoiseshell, another butterfly that is about now in good numbers.

10th Tree mallow is still in flower in rocky places along the coast and on the edges of beaches. *Malva arborea* is a stately native plant, a metre and more high with green-grey, felted leaves and pinky-mauve, silky flowers with dark centres. It belongs to the same family as the garden hollyhock, and has similarly open-faced blooms. Despite its 'tree' moniker, it is usually biennial, flowering in its second year and then dying. It thrives in some seabird colonies, fed a rich diet by the abundant guano deposits. Its rampant growth can be a hindrance to ground- and hole-nesting birds such as terns and puffins. On Rockabill, the two islands off the coast of north County Dublin, where there is an internationally important roseate tern colony, wardens and volunteers chop down stands of tree mallow before the nesting season starts. At one time, the soft, furry foliage provided a remedy for sprains: it was boiled up and applied as a poultice. In Jersey, tree mallow was grown at the end of cottage gardens, next to the privy, where its leaves were easily harvested to use as toilet paper.

11th It is cranefly season, when the giant, winged insects come inside to prance around on gangly legs, jigging across ceilings and clattering into lampshades. They are far more graceful outdoors, when their long limbs – which give them the common name of daddy-longlegs – hang down languorously as they drift over fields and lawns. These lengthy appendages allow them to keep balance while perched on swaying grass blades. Craneflies' large size and many graspable bits make them an easy target for insect-eating birds, but they have the life-saving ability to shed legs when snatched by a predator. It is not uncommon to see a four- or five-legged individual. Their lifespan is only a few days, during which time they do not feed. Their sole aim is to mate and lay eggs. The dark brownish-grey larvae have tough, hide-like skins and are known as leatherjackets. They spend nine or ten months underground, when they eat the roots of plants such as grass and grains. Lawn zealots hate them, but they are an important food source for birds, including starlings.

12th The dunlin, the smallest of the common waders on our shorelines, will be visiting in large numbers over the coming months. Those appearing now are mostly passing through on their way south from Greenland to their winter grounds in west Africa. Another contingent, from Scandinavia and Siberia, will arrive soon to spend the winter here, often in sizeable flocks. Counts of over ten thousand have been recorded in the Shannon Estuary in County Clare and Dundalk Bay in County Louth. The dumpy-bodied dunlin is about the size of a starling, with black legs, a black, down-curved beak and appealingly large eyes. Adult winter plumage is plain grey above with a white belly, while first year birds are more patterned – a mixture of brown, chestnut and grey with a buff, slightly-spotted chest. The dunlin is often seen with the golden plover, and was once known as the plover's page. It was recently declared a red-listed species, at the highest level of conservation concern. The wintering population has decreased dramatically, while the range of the summer breeding population (already headed back to north Africa and southern Europe) has contracted to just a few areas, mostly upland blanket bog in the west and northwest.

13th Native meadow saffron is in flower in just a handful of spots. Although this mauvey-pink-flowered bulb occurs throughout Britain, on this island it is found only in the Nore and Barrow River valleys in the southeast. Its habitat is damp grassland. Robert Lloyd Praeger reported it as 'widespread' in that area in 1922, but now it is one of seven Irish plant species listed as critically endangered. (The others are divided sedge, serrated wintergreen, cottonweed, rough poppy, meadow saxifrage and marsh saxifrage.) In Irish it is *cróch an fhómhair*, which translates as autumn crocus. Its Latin name (*Colchicum autumnale*) demonstrates that it is a different plant genus, even though it looks somewhat like the crocuses we grow in our gardens. Because it is poisonous in all its parts, it was traditionally unwelcome to owners of grazing animals. Agriculture and development have been its enemies. The leaves appear in spring and have withered away by the time the pale flowers appear. Its starkness has conferred on it the popular name of 'naked ladies'. In France, where it is also native, it is known as '*cul tout nu*' which – with admirable French directness – means 'bare arse'.

14th Fly agaric, in woodlands now, is the white-warted, red toadstool of children's fairytales. It is a mycorrhizal associate of certain trees, including birch, spruce, fir and pine. Tree and mushroom form a cooperative alliance, which benefits each organism: the roots donate their spare sugars to the underground strands of the fungus (the hyphae), while they, in turn, feed water and nutrients back to the tree. *Amanita muscaria* is native to Europe and north America, but has been introduced to Australia, South Africa and New Zealand with pine seedlings. At one time it was used to poison flies. The toxins, while not usually fatal to humans, can have extremely unpleasant effects. However, in 1897 Colonel Achilles de Vecchi, an Italian diplomat in Washington D.C., died after eating 'considerable quantities' according to a report in the *New York Times*. He and fellow mushroom-lover Dr D. J. Kelley were attempting to prove that the 'virulent properties ... had been over estimated'. Both men became violently ill, and while Dr Kelley recovered, de Vecchi, 'who was said to be an Italian count', was less fortunate.

15th Yarrow is brightening grassy roadsides: its small white plates of flowers are offered up on knee-high stems clad in feathery leaves. In fact, it has been blooming for some months, but it is more noticeable now as many other plants have finished flowering and are well into their seeding cycle. Its late blooms with their flat, accessible flowers make it invaluable for a wide range of insects, including bees, flies, butterflies, moths and beetles. Despite its dainty appearance, yarrow is tough: its deep roots give it great tenacity and allow it to compete with grass and to resist herbicides. It also has creeping, underground stems (rhizomes) which regenerate after mowing. The botanical name, *Achillea millefolium*, honours the Trojan hero, Achilles, who used it as a remedy to heal wounds, having learned of its properties from his mentor, Chiron the centaur. In Irish, yarrow is *athair thalún*, father of the earth, a name that suggests its importance in mythology and folklore. It is said that if you sew some sprigs into your clothes, you will be protected from disease.

16th It's that time of year when big, athletic spiders scurry at speed through our homes, an unnerving clatter of elbows and knees moving faster than the eye can follow. The most frequently seen is the so-called giant house spider (*Eratigena atrica*). The giant part is entirely true, but it lives outdoors in drier habitats as well as inside. Males mature in the autumn of their second year, and begin roaming around looking for a mate, which is why they are so visible now. The females usually stay in their webs, a messy sheet of strands slung across a corner or in a niche. If a male approaches and she likes the look of him, he is allowed to mate. The process is not what you might expect. There is no conjoining of intimate parts. Instead, he uses his pedipalps, the bulbous appendages located in front of his first pair of legs, to transfer his sperm into her epigynal opening on the underside of her abdomen. The resulting eggs hatch before winter and the spiderlings overwinter as juveniles.

17th While summer flowers are finishing, one curious native is starting to bloom. The Killarney strawberry tree opens its first buds in autumn and keeps producing them for three to four months, when they supply nectar and pollen to the winter-flying, buff-tailed bumblebee. The creamy, tubular flowers are gathered into clusters and are the same shape as those of its relative, bell heather. The tree, which grows on the edges of oak woods, is indigenous to Cork and Kerry and to Lough Gill in County Sligo. It is an anomaly, occurring in Ireland, but skipping Britain and northern Europe. Its other native territories include areas around the Mediterranean and Adriatic coasts, and on the Iberian peninsula. The warty, spherical fruits take the best part of a year to ripen, when they attain a rich scarlet-crimson. They are borne at the same time as the flowers, making this evergreen tree very ornamental. Although the fruits were regularly eaten at one time, they are quite unpalatable: the latter part of the botanical name, *Arbutus unedo*, reflects this, translating as 'I eat one'. Arbutus timber was an essential ingredient in Victorian 'Killarney ware', elaborately inlaid pieces of small furniture and items such as bookends and writing boxes, often sold to tourists.

18th Barn swallows are leaving us. Many have already left their nest sites and are on their way south, stopping off at insect-rich wetlands to feed up before setting out across the water. Tacumshin Lake in south County Wexford is a favoured spot: ten thousand swallows and martins may roost in the reed beds on September nights. When they make the 10,000-kilometre journey back to sub-Saharan Africa, swallows fly about 300 kilometres a day, travelling at 27–35 kilometres per hour. Unlike many migrating birds, they are daytime fliers, as they are able to feed on the wing as they go. Usually birds forage during daylight hours and migrate at night. Before crossing areas with few insects, such as seas and the Sahara Desert, swallows try to put on just enough fat to last them until the next meal. Two-thirds of this year's fledglings will succumb to starvation, exhaustion or bad weather. Those that survive can live to a good age – up to sixteen years. In 1912, a leg ring from a British swallow was recovered in South Africa. This was the first proof that these tiny birds migrate so far south. Before it was known that swallows migrated, some people believed that they hibernated in the mud in wetlands. The presence of dead swallows in the reed-beds where they had gathered helped fuel this myth.

19th Street trees are starting to change into their autumn outfits. The leaves of limes and chestnuts (both horse and Spanish) are among the first to show colour – or more correctly, to lose colour. At the end of the growing season, chlorophyll breaks down and reveals carotenoids, yellow and peachy pigments. These glowing colours were already present in the leaf, but were masked by the green chlorophyll. The red and purple autumn tints on some trees are anthocyanins, manufactured by excess sugars that get trapped in the leaves. A few cherries, mountain ash and garden trees such as stag's-horn sumac are beginning to show smatterings of crimson and scarlet, but the main red flush is still weeks off. The most vibrant colour is achieved when the days are bright and sunny and the nights are cold. During a mild and moist season, the display is more muted. In a good year, there are trees sporting fiery colours until well into November.

20th Look for brent geese flying and honking overhead. Unlike other geese, they do not regularly arrange themselves in V-formation. They are just as likely to form long, straggling, ever-shifting ribbons. The first flocks arrived from their summer home in the Canadian High Arctic in the latter half of August, but the main influx is this month. They travel as family units, with the adults staying with their young until the spring, schooling them in the disciplines of migration and winter foraging. They come via Greenland and Iceland to spend the winter here. Ireland hosts around thirty thousand migrants, the bulk of the wintering population of the pale-bellied subspecies of this small goose (*Branta bernicla hrota*). A lesser number fly to Britain and France. The majority of our visitors congregate for some weeks at the eelgrass-rich Strangford Lough in County Down before dispersing to other parts of the island. They return to the same sites year after year, mostly bays and estuaries around the coast. As the food becomes depleted along the shore, they move inland to feed on grassland, including pastures, playing fields and parks.

21st Gardeners are grateful to Michaelmas daisies for blooming in the month of September, when many plants are winding down for the year. Their wild relative, the sea aster, is also in full flight, with clusters of yellow-centred mauve flowers, an important source of nectar for late-flying butterflies. The blooms are borne in profusion on fleshy-leaved plants that are between 30 and 100 centimetres tall. *Aster tripolium* is native to northern Europe and is common along the coast of Ireland. It is a halophyte: tolerant of saline water or soils. It grows in salt marshes with its roots in salty water, and it is also at home on cliffs and in rocky places on the seashore. There are recent records of sea asters appearing along the margins of roads that have been treated with salt. In parts of the Netherlands, *zulte* is a delicacy. The leaves, which are harvested in spring and at the beginning of summer, are served lightly cooked.

22nd If you're out for a walk in an area of heath, grassland or open woodland, look for large and handsome hairy caterpillars sunning themselves on the path. If you see one that is finger-sized and dark-brown with orange accents, it is the final instar (phase) of the fox moth larva. This is one of several caterpillars known colloquially as a 'hairy molly'. The latter half of the name comes from the Irish *mala*, meaning an eyebrow. Folklore collected in Tipperary in the 1930s noted: 'When the hairy-molly crosses the road rain is near.' In several counties, the unlucky caterpillars were a cure for whooping cough. In County Mayo, one was directed to 'catch a hairy molly, tie the little animal in a red cloth and put it round the person's neck who is bad with the cough'. On warm days in autumn and winter the caterpillar feeds on bramble, heather, bilberry and meadowsweet. In spring, it pupates for about four weeks, after which the adult emerges. Males have a wingspan of around fifty millimetres and are a warm, fox brown. They have elegant 'combed' antennae, with a feathery look. These complex filaments sense the pheromones given off by unmated females, and allow males to detect a potential mate's chemical signals from a field's length away. Female fox moths are a little larger and greyer and have unadorned antennae.

23rd Some years there is an abundance of wild fruits in hedgerows and field margins; branches are heavy with gleaming blackberries, rose hips, rowan berries and others. Folk wisdom says that such a generous bounty heralds a hard winter ahead, and that trees and shrubs are stocking nature's larder for the birds and other hungry animals. Instead, the truth is that the profusion of fruits is a result of a happy confluence of factors. Flowers appeared in spring as usual, and escaped being damaged by wind, rain, frost or birds. Plentiful pollinators, such as bees, hoverflies, flies, moths and butterflies, emerged punctually to carry pollen to stigmas and thereby cause fertilisation. Rain fell at the right time to swell the berries, and sunshine arrived on schedule to ripen them. During very hot and sunny summers, some fruits – blackberries and rowan, for example – ripen earlier than usual, and many may be stripped from their branches before the winter comes. In such years the abundance may be short-lived.

24th Among the many birds on the move now are meadow pipits. This robin-sized species looks like a miniature thrush, with speckled breast and brownish back – although it is not related. The flocks of tens and even hundreds of 'mippits' (as they are known by birders) passing through at present are mostly migrants from northern Europe, making a stop on their way to warmer parts of the continent. Some, arriving later, may choose to winter here. Our own resident meadow pipits breed in summer in rough, grassy places and raised bogs (giving them one of their many names, 'bog lark'). In late autumn, when food becomes scarce, upland meadow pipits move to lower ground, where there are more insects to feed on. Some of the Irish birds coming to their winter quarters will be exhausted after a nesting season during which they fed monstrously large, incessantly hungry chicks – completely unrelated to them. Meadow pipits are most often chosen as unwitting foster parents by cuckoos. One of their vernacular names in Ulster is 'cuckoo's maid'.

25th Coastal plants are robust, with a dogged ability to seed in hostile places. Make your way along any older pier or promenade and you will find specialised species that are engineered to withstand wind, salt and high light levels. Most have a ground-hugging habit and leathery or succulent foliage. Sea cliffs are their usual habitat, but the crevices in maritime masonry offer similar conditions. They trap morsels of decaying seaweed and other nutritious detritus, providing a tiny foothold and a spartan meal for a windblown seed.

The prettiest and daintiest of them all are the pink, five-petalled and golden-stamened sea-spurreys (*Spergularia*), with fleshy, linear leaves. Often they share space with buck's-horn plantain (*Plantago coronopus*), with its flattened green sunbursts of jagged leaves and dull batons of flower. The oraches (*Atriplex*) also take advantage of the same crevices. These have arrow-shaped leaves and nubby flower heads, the kind of plant you'd never notice if you weren't looking.

26th Turnstones are curious little waders no larger than a blackbird, common on stony beaches and seaweedy rocks. Their stocky bodies seem permanently tipped forward on sturdy, salmon-pink legs. Heads down, they rush ever onward, intently flicking over bits of seaweed and – true to their name – turning stones to search for invertebrates. When disturbed, they skitter along hurriedly, reluctant to take off until utterly necessary. Their mottled, black-and-brown upper parts allow them to blend seamlessly with pebbles or rocks, and they become visible only when they take off and expose snowy underparts and graphic white patterns on back and wings. It's hard to believe that such homely-looking birds are long-distance travellers, but they arrive from northeast Canada and Greenland in autumn to spend the winter here. Younger birds, non-breeders, are often present in summer, while migrants from northern Europe pass through in late summer and spring. Turnstones are able to adapt to human habitats and foods, perhaps because their usual diet of intertidal fare can be scarce. They have been known to eat fish and chips, as well as grain spilled on docks.

27th Woody nightshade (also known as bittersweet) is a straggly vine, with lax stems that weave and clamber through other plants. It grows in many places, including hedgerows, ditches, woodland edges and wasteland. Where councils have stopped spraying, it appears along roadways and in wall crevices. Before it flowers, *Solanum dulcamara* is unremarkable, with dark-green, oval leaves and an untidy appearance. Now, however, it is gleaming with bright pops of colour: deep purple and yellow flowers and shiny green berries that ripen to radiant red. It is closely related to the potato, and a little more distantly to the notoriously poisonous deadly nightshade, but is not as toxic. In 1772, however, John Rutty, physician and naturalist, noted in *An Essay towards the Natural History of the County of Dublin*: 'Sir John Floyer reports that he gave thirty of these berries to a Dog, and that in three days it died mad.' Traditionally it had many uses. Caleb Threlkeld, in his 1726 *Synopsis Stirpium Hibernacarum* writes: 'The Leaves and Twigs are commended by some against the Dropsy, Jaundice, and King's-Evil [scrofula]; it is an Evacuator of Bile, the Leaves are profitable against the Itchy Swellings of Hands and Feet.'

28th Flocks of blue tits are hanging around gardens now, boisterous gangs that are sometimes joined by coal and long-tailed tits and the occasional goldcrest. The breeding season is over and blue tits no longer defend their territories. Instead, they band together into roving flocks and range through woodlands and gardens. They combine great agility with strong claws, and are able to exploit more food sources than other birds. They are equally able to cling to a peanut feeder or to dangle from the end of a branch where the buds hide overwintering aphids. Wordsworth immortalised the nimbleness of the 'blue-cap', 'that giddy Sprite', in his poem 'The Kitten and the Falling Leaves':

Hung with head towards the ground,
Flutter'd, perch'd, into a round
Bound himself, and then unbound;
Lithest, gaudiest Harlequin!
Prettiest Tumbler ever seen!

In the days when bottled milk was delivered daily to doorsteps, blue tits habitually pecked through the foil caps to steal the cream that had settled on top. They even learned to ignore skimmed milk, which had a different coloured cap. Blue tits have been recorded in over 98 per cent of Irish gardens.

29th The leaves on some horse chestnut trees, especially along the east and south coasts, have been turning brown and falling early. This is often the work of a tiny moth (less than half a centimetre long), a recent arrival in Ireland. The brown-and-silver horse-chestnut leaf miner (*Cameraria ohridella*) was found in south Dublin in July 2013 and has since been recorded in several regions. The minute larvae feed on leaf tissue, creating 'mines' under the surface: pale markings that turn rust and brown. They pupate here, sandwiched between the thin layers of leaf. When the adult moths break out, they sometimes leave a dark pupal case on the leaf. The insect has spread throughout Europe since first being observed in Macedonia in the late 1970s. Researchers studying trees in Bern, Switzerland, noted several species of tit feeding on the larvae, and suggested siting nest boxes among chestnut trees as natural protection. In 2018, in the UK, analysis of brown long-eared bat droppings showed that the second largest component (16.53 per cent) was the horse-chestnut leaf miner. Brown long-eared bats are intolerant of densely populated areas, so could not be lured into urban trees, but blue tits have lived happily next to our species for hundreds of years.

30th The common puffball is relatively frequent now and is easy to identify. It appears in clusters in grass alongside woodland paths or in clearings. The individual mushrooms or fruiting bodies (their purpose is to spread spores) are white, shading to mocha. They look like bundles of miniature cartoonish clubs, covered in goosebumps. The stipples break off regularly, leaving pure white dots, like minuscule pockmarks. The flesh, which is known as the gleba, is white and spongy – and edible when young. (It's wise, however, not to indulge unless the mushroom has been identified by an expert.) Puffballs are so called because when ripe the spores are ejected through a spout called an ostiole in the centre of the fruiting body. Drops of rain or drips from trees exert enough pressure to discharge a puff. The common puffball belongs to the genus *Lycoperdon*, a name derived from the Ancient Greek. *Lycos* means wolf, while 'perdon' is from *perdomai*, to break wind. So, wolf farts are in season now.

October

1st For most of the year, our native spindle is almost invisible, merging into hedgerows or patches of scrubby vegetation in wild places. Around the beginning of this month, though, this large shrub bounces into the limelight by producing highly ornate, psychedelic-looking fruits. The four-part capsules of *Euonymus europaeus* are a shocking pink, and they open to reveal seeds covered in bright orange flesh – a colour combination lifted straight off a trippy 1960s album cover. Soon the unremarkable, ovate green leaves join the party by turning a vivid crimson. The fruits, inedible for humans, are popular with tits, finches, thrushes and other birds. The leaves are a larval food for the holly blue butterfly and several moths, including the spindle ermine and magpie. The latter is a striking moth; its white wings have a dappled pattern of black and amber dots, like ink marks on blotting paper. The wood of *feoras* (in Irish) is hard and dense, and was used for making small, precise items such as spindles for wool spinning, knitting needles and pegs (in parts of Ireland it was known as peg-wood). In 1772, John Rutty noted that spindle tree or 'prick-wood' 'supplies skewers for butchers, and makes good Tooth-pickers, and is used by Watch-makers for cleaning their watches'.

2nd Those of us who are unnerved by the huge, dark house spiders that race across our floors in this season have an inconspicuous ally in the dainty long-bodied cellar spider. *Pholcus phalangioides* is a pale, barely-there arachnid with lanky, thread-like legs and a body resembling a small grain of rice. It is one of three invertebrates known as a daddy-longlegs: the others are the harvestman and the cranefly. This ghostly creature inhabits not just cellars, but undusted corners of houses and niches under furniture where it weaves an airy, tangled web. Its diet is varied: besides eating other spiders, it consumes insects, woodlice and other invertebrates. In times of scarcity, it turns on its own species. It is a 'synanthrope', a species that benefits from humans – in this case, because we have provided it with a congenial place to live and breed. When threatened, it sways back and forth quickly to become a blur, thus presenting a difficult target to a potential foe. The female carries her eggs in a silk package under her body. When they hatch, she minds the spiderlings for about nine days.

3rd Whitebeams, smallish trees of rocky places, woodland edges and suburban streets, are bearing small clusters of red berries that look similar to rose hips. And indeed, they are members of the huge rose family, a clan that gives us the greatest number of autumn fruiters, including apple, pear, plum, hawthorn, sloe, cherry and mountain ash. Whitebeams are most closely related to the last: both are members of the same genus, *Sorbus*. The 'white' in the name comes from the pale backs to the handsome, relatively large, oval leaves: a light breeze is enough to send a silvery shimmer through a tree's canopy. The 'beam' is from the Old English for tree (similar to the German *baum*), and it occurs only in one other species, hornbeam. Most whitebeams we see are *Sorbus aria*, a native of much of Europe, including parts of Ireland. We also have our own endemic whitebeam (found nowhere else), *S. hibernica*, with a slightly different leaf shape. It is mainly present on limestone in the midlands and west. In Irish, whitebeam is *fionncholl* – white hazel – because the foliage is not dissimilar to that of hazel. Irish whitebeam is *fionncholl gaelach*.

4th Adult shieldbugs are about, sunning themselves on warm walls and stones, or even on windows. They will hibernate over the winter and emerge in spring to mate. They are unlike any other insect and are well-named. Their bodies resemble mediaeval shields: chunky, robust and ornate. Those you are likely to see now are the green shieldbug (entirely green with a dark base where the wing membranes overlap) and the hawthorn shieldbug, a handsome thing with bold green-and-brown heraldic markings. They are true bugs, with tube-like mouthparts (the rostrum) adapted for sucking. Most are vegetarian, feeding on plant sap, but a few are carnivorous, latching on to the larvae of other insects. Shieldbugs are relatively sedentary and make excellent specimens for studying with a hand lens or in a jam jar. If you are capturing insects to examine, put a piece of tissue in the jar for them to cling to and set them free after a few minutes. Shieldbugs are also known as stink bugs: when they feel threatened they release a malodorous liquid from glands behind the first pair of legs. Our species are not as foul-smelling as those from warmer climates, but there is a definite whiff of something acrid if you upset one.

5th There is a pretty little purple mushroom around now with the irresistible name of amethyst deceiver. Look for it under beech and oak trees in woodlands. At its tallest, *Laccaria amethystina* is half the height of your hand, with a slim stem and a soft, suede cap – neat and pert when young and undulating and spreading when older. The deceiver part of its handle comes from its relative, the common deceiver (*L. laccata*), which occurs in a flummoxing range of colours, including brick-red, salmon-pink, chestnut-brown and pale tan, depending on habitat and age. The amethyst version is likewise prone to pigmentation changes: violet when young, lighter and more beige as it ages. Orange-peel fungus is also in season. It is easy to mistake for a discarded orange peel, especially as it often appears along walking trails. It sometimes crops up on newly disturbed ground, so look for it on recently made banks and lawns. In younger specimens, the underside of *Aleuria aurantia* is pale and felted, just like the peel of its namesake. The fruiting bodies start out cup-shaped, often with a fold, and as they age they split and become more splayed.

6th Yew trees are spangled with their curious berries. The pinkish-red fruits have a matte surface and a regular, round aperture, which gives them a beadlike, manufactured appearance. Yew is highly poisonous, and ingesting it can be fatal. But its leaves also contain powerful anti-cancer compounds from which the drug paclitaxel (commonly known as Taxol) is made. The name derives from yew's botanical name, *Taxus baccata*. The fruits, however, are harmless to birds, and are a favourite with thrushes, who gorge on them with impunity. The fleshy part, known as the aril, is free from taxine, the toxic alkaloid compound. When birds eat the fruits, the poisonous seeds pass intact through their digestive tracts, perhaps to germinate and produce another yew tree. In Brehon law, the yew was one of the 'nobles of the wood', and there were severe penalties for illegally felling or damaging a tree. The hard wood was prized for bows, spears and household items.

7th Whooper swans are arriving from Iceland. The first few usually fly in during September, but the main influx of the winter population arrives this month. They move through the air on powerful wings (with a span of up to 2.4 metres), honking loudly with their old-style bicycle-horn calls. The Irish name, *eala ghlórach*, means 'noisy swan'. The birds have extra-long windpipes to add depth and volume to their voices. They will continue to show up during the coming weeks, taking advantage of our mild climate's fertile foraging grounds. They feed during daytime, mainly on pastures and farmland, retreating at dusk to the safety of wetlands. Over fifteen thousand spend the winter in Ireland, around 45 per cent of the European population. The whooper swan has a yellow-and-black bill (as does the rarer Bewick's swan), while that of our resident mute swan is mainly orange. Although they are one of the heaviest flying birds – adult males can be over eleven kilograms – whoopers have been observed at enormously high altitudes. In 1967, a pilot spotted a flock flying over the Hebrides at a height of 8,200 metres.

8 th Pheasant berry is coming to the end of its blooming period, but its dangling inflorescences will be decorative for some months longer. The white, tubular flowers that hang out from claret-coloured, hood-like bracts are being replaced by glossy, purple-black berries. This straggly Himalayan native was introduced to cultivation in Britain and Ireland in 1824 as an ornamental shrub, but was soon widely planted as cover for game in country estates. Landowners delighted in its attributes: enough vigour to compete with native plants, rapid growth to clothe a large area quickly, plentiful shelter and berries to feed game birds. In time, however, Himalayan honeysuckle (as it is also known) became too much of a good thing. It grows readily from discarded fragments and its seeds are spread over a wide area by birds. *Leycesteria formosa* was first recorded in the wild in 1955 and is now deemed a medium-impact invasive species. The berries – when ripe to the point of near mushiness – are edible and are said to taste of toffee.

9 th Small tortoiseshell butterflies are still about, although scarce. At this point, their orange-and-black, Hallowe'en-esque wings are a little threadbare, and the neon blue spots along the edges are likely to be frayed. These stragglers, the second brood to hatch this year, are preparing to go into hibernation for the chilly months. Late flowers such as Michaelmas daisies, sedums and the farmer's enemy, ragwort, supply nectar in this season. *Aglais urticae* overwinters – often communally – in sheds or garages. In colder houses, they sometimes secrete themselves in the folds of curtains in rarely used rooms. Warm winter days may see individuals waking up and flitting about incongruously. In March or April they emerge for good, and after mating, the females select patches of young nettles in sunny locations. There they lay 60–100 eggs, which look like piles of miniature gooseberries. The small tortoiseshell is native to Europe and temperate Asia. It is nearly indistinguishable from its ancestor (*Aglais karaganica*), which exists as a mid-Miocene fossil, about fifteen million years old.

10th Now, while oaks are bearing acorns, is a good time to learn the difference between our two native species, the pedunculate and sessile oaks. Known as the English oak across the water, the pedunculate kind (*Quercus robur*) bears acorns with a stalk. Those on the sessile oak (*Q. petraea*) are stalkless: sessile means to be seated or sedentary, from the Latin *sedere*. This species, the national tree of Ireland, is native to more mountainous counties (*petraea* means of rocky places) such as Wicklow, Donegal and Kerry. The pedunculate oak is associated more with the heavy soil of the midlands. The tallest oak in Ireland is the so-called Squire's Walking Stick at Tullynally in County Westmeath, a ramrod-straight tree of over thirty-four metres, planted around 1745. It was one of a dozen saplings planted by the first Baron Longford to provide timber for the British Navy, but it was never felled. Stand under an oak in this season, and you're likely to get pelted with acorns as jackdaws, rooks and jays knock them down while foraging.

11th Warm autumn days often see the air filled with hundreds of miniature *Linyphiidae* spiders floating on strands of silk, like eensy-weensy balloonists. We have around two hundred species in this genus, including the shiny and tiny black 'money spiders', which are supposed to bring luck and prosperity when they land on you. Recent research by biologists at the University of Bristol has shown that ballooning spiders depend on electrostatic charges in the atmosphere to hoist themselves upwards. When conditions are right, sensory hairs (trichobothria) on the legs react by lifting up (in the same way your hair lifts when rubbed with a balloon). The spider then stands on tiptoe, points its abdomen upwards and releases silk filaments that carry it aloft by static electricity. Some journeys may be only a few metres, but if the spider catches a breeze, it may travel hundreds of kilometres, and at up to four kilometres high.

12th October often brings fierce and damaging storms. Trees still have plenty of leaves, and these can act as sails, catching and amplifying the wind's force. Forests and woodlands can sustain a lot of damage in this month. Yet, the wind-thrown casualties and debris support an abundance of wildlife. Deadwood is an essential ingredient in a healthy forest ecosystem: about a fifth of woodland creatures depend on it during their life cycle. Veteran trees with some rot or damage, rotten stumps, and the poetic 'standing dead' and 'fallen dead' (as they are known in arboriculture) all provide different habitats. Mosses, liverworts, lichen, fungi and ferns colonise the material, and in turn offer habitats and food for many animals, great and small. Saproxylic (associated with deadwood) invertebrate species are in their hundreds, and include earthworms, slugs, millipedes, centipedes, spiders, moths, wasps, bees, flies and around two hundred beetles. Hedgehogs, otters, red squirrels, pine martens and bats also depend on deadwood. Many birds likewise rely on it, including one of Ireland's most recent colonists, the great spotted woodpecker.

13th Horse chestnuts are falling and peeping shinily from their green, spiny casings. These, of course, are conkers, the essential components for the game of the same name that hardly anyone plays any more. In times past, conkers and even 'conquers' was an important autumn pursuit for boys, and latterly, girls. Chestnuts were pierced with nails and long strings attached. Players took turns trying to bash their opponents' chestnuts to bits. Various means such as soaking in vinegar and smoking in the fire were used to harden the nuts and make them more lethal. Chestnuts were used to make necklaces and other objects, including baskets for dolls, whistles and pipes. They also had healing powers. An account collected in County Cavan in the 1930s says: 'The remedy for rheumatism was to get a chestnut and carry it in the pocket. When the chestnut was withered the rheumatism would be gone.' In 1772, John Rutty reported that they were 'efficacious in whitening hemp, flax or cloth' and for making starch. Horse chestnuts (unlike the sweet or Spanish chestnut) are not edible, and the starch was not for culinary purposes. In recent years researchers have experimented with making plastic substitutes from horse chestnut starch.

14th For the past few years, this month has seen numerous strandings of Portuguese men o' war on the coast of Ireland. They lie on beaches like curious, abandoned polythene bags in iridescent tones that shift from pink to violet to blue. Although this marine organism resembles a jellyfish, it is a siphonophore: an interdependent colony of polyps. Each is specialised for a different task such as flotation, hunting, digestion and breeding. The bloated, gas-filled float (the pneumatophore) gives the organism its name, as it looks like a fighting ship under full sail. The tentacles range from ten to thirty metres in length and are armed with venomous, stinging nematocysts. The toxins paralyse fish, which are then consumed. Even when a Portuguese man o' war is dead, the tentacles remain potent and can still deliver venom. Research published in 2017 from a joint project by the National University of Ireland, Galway and the University of Hawaii-Manoa suggests that the most effective treatment for stings is to rinse with vinegar, which deactivates the stinging cells, and to apply a hot pack (at 45°C) or immerse in hot water.

15th The dandelion-like flowers of smooth sow-thistle have been popping out in gardens, fields and waste places since late spring. In mild areas plants may flower into December. *Sonchus oleraceus* is an opportunistic wild plant (or weed, in the eyes of some) of arable land. It is rather tall and thin (30–80 centimetres high) and has a distinctive blue-grey, matte sheen to the leaves. The plant looks a little over-lanky and wishy-washy, and indeed, the hollow stems break easily. The seeds, like those of dandelions, are dispersed on pappi, little hairy parachutes. Small birds, such as finches and blue tits, eat the seeds. Plants often overwinter, when they act as a refuge for aphids. These, in turn, will provide sustenance for birds and other insect-eaters. The leaves of sow-thistle are edible, and can be steamed like spinach, according to several sources. They are likely to be unpalatable at this time of the year, however. A vernacular name in Ireland is 'swine's thistle', as the plant was used to feed pigs. The related prickly sow-thistle (*S. asper*) with shiny, greener leaves, is also in bloom, although it is reaching the end of its flowering cycle.

16th Listen carefully at night and you may hear intermittent, plaintive 'tseeeeep' notes overhead. Needle-thin, but far-carrying, these are the calls of redwings flying above. Although they sound lonely, the calls are actually the way the birds stay in touch with their fellow travellers, flying under cover of darkness in order to escape predators. These visitors, from Iceland, Scandinavia and the Faroe Islands, are our winter thrushes – so called because they spend the cold months here, along with their relatives, fieldfares and migrant song thrushes, mistle thrushes and blackbirds. The redwing is slightly smaller than the song thrush, with a short tail that gives it a more dumpy profile. It is named for the rusty patches on the underwings and flanks, but these can be difficult to spot. Instead, look for the distinctive cream eyebrow (known as a supercilium), a feature that gives great definition to the face. *Deargán sneachta*, or the 'red one of the snow' will spend the winter here on farmland (often in huge flocks, along with fieldfares) and in gardens, feeding on earthworms and on fruits such as cotoneaster, hawthorn and rowan.

17th Heathers are still in flower in bogs and on heaths and mountainsides. There are three Irish species that you are likely to encounter. Most common is ling heather

(*Calluna vulgaris*), the dominant plant on dry mountainsides and heaths. This has tiny flowers, each with visibly separate pinky-mauve, petal-looking parts (in fact, a mixture of petals and sepals). Bell heather (*Erica cinerea*) is often in its company, and has larger, brighter flowers that are distinctly tubular in appearance. Also larger and tubular are the flowers of cross-leaved heath (*E. tetralix*). This last species is confined to wetter areas. Between them, these three heathers support dozens of insects. They provide nectar for bees and other pollinators, and are the food for the larvae of many moths. In summer, heather-rich habitats offer shelter to ground-nesting birds such as curlew, skylark, meadow pipit, red grouse and golden plover. Traditionally, the plants were used for many purposes. These included brewing beer and dyeing wool with the shoots and flowers. The branches, meanwhile, were used to make brooms, lobster pots and other objects.

18th Hedgehogs are going into hibernation shortly. At present they are feeding intensively at night on invertebrates (including slugs, earthworms, moth larvae, spiders and beetles) and on fungi and fallen fruit. The layers of fat will help sustain them during the cold weather. Instead of sleeping non-stop during the winter, most wake a number of times when they may move to another hibernation site – or hibernaculum. Researchers have tracked different hedgehogs using the same hibernacula, although not at the same time. They emerge for good in spring between mid-March and mid-May. The hedgehog is not native to Ireland. It was introduced in the twelfth century or earlier, possibly as a food source or as a means of pest control. The unfortunate *gráinneog* (the ugly little one) was widely used in folk medicine: a soup was recommended as a cure for whooping cough, while a jawbone or tooth would sort out a toothache. Hedgehogs may hibernate under a compost heap or in a pile of leaves. If you have a garden pond, ensure that there is a stepped side so they can scramble out if they tumble in.

19th Rosebay willowherb, which began to go to fluffy seed two months ago, is still brandishing its elongated flower stems. They are mostly bare, but on some there are remnants of white floss, flattened and tangled by rain and wind. In some cases, on poorer ground, the willowherb's leaves are turning bright red before dropping. Another plant that sometimes displays brilliant autumn colour is the invasive Japanese knotweed. Foxgloves occupy similar terrain – waste lots, hillsides, disturbed ground and the edges of forestry – and while they finished flowering during the summer, they will carry their tall, dried seedheads for many months. Sheep's-bit (*Jasione montana*) is a small, easily-missed plant, still in flower in rocky places and on mountain sides. It has beautiful blue flowers, like soft, tasselled bobbles. Look for it in little hollows, often surrounded by rough grass. Tread carefully, though, as the white-spotted pug moth or its very rare relative, the jasione pug moth, may be pupating in the soil at its feet.

20th We're in peak breeding season for the red deer, Ireland's largest native land animal – and only native deer. Healthy stags can weigh up to 250 kilograms and stand 1.4 metres at the shoulder; hinds are smaller: up to 140 kilograms in weight and 1.05 metres in height. For most of the year, adult males and females live separate lives, but for these few weeks in autumn they come together to mate – for the 'rut'. Mature stags gather interested hinds by bellowing and posturing. They are constantly vigilant, mustering their females together and checking if they are in heat. The deep, resonant roars serve also to warn off other males. Rival stags fight by shoving their antlered heads together until the weaker opponent is driven off. The famous red deer of Killarney National Park have an ancient lineage. Genetic testing has shown that they are the direct descendants of a herd present in Ireland since Neolithic times, at least five thousand years ago. Red deer in other areas were rendered extinct during the Great Famine, and were reintroduced from England and Scotland. The name Fiadh comes from the Irish for deer, while Oscar and Oisín are from 'os', a literary word meaning deer.

21st Most thistles are well into their woolly headed phase and are dispatching their seeds to fresh territories on hairy parachutes. The magnificent spear thistle, however, is still in flower. This is the boldest of our several thistles, standing proud and tall (up to 1.5 metres) and crowned with elegant flowers of vibrant magenta, each crowding out of a spiny, grey, egg-shaped bud. The pale-backed leaves are jaggedly cut, with each tip ending in a vicious spike – the 'spear' of the common name. In Northern Ireland it was known as the bull thistle, and in parts of the east as buck-thrissle. This, *Cirsium vulgare*, is the Scotch thistle of heraldry (although some argue that the honour goes to *Onopordum acanthium*, the cotton thistle, rarely found in the wild in Scotland). Spear thistle is full of nectar now. Later, the seeds will feed goldfinches. It is also the larval plant for seven different moths.

22nd. The goldcrest, with its dapper amber-and-black head-stripe, is Ireland's tiniest bird. An older name is the golden-crested wren. Although unrelated, it is superficially similar in size and colouring to the wren. It weighs between five and seven grams, the same as a wine-bottle cork. The usual home of *an cíor bhuí*, as it is known in Irish, is among mature conifers, but it often visits gardens in autumn and winter, sometimes mingling with other small birds such as tits. Some of our visitors at this time of the year are migrants, seeking refuge from colder parts of Europe. There are many reports of exhausted and confused birds landing on ships at sea. On land, goldcrests are restless birds, constantly on the move, searching for spiders and insects among evergreen plants and in bark crevices. In colder weather they must feed continually to maintain body weight. During harsh winters their population takes a dire hit, but numbers gradually build up again. As a rule, goldcrests don't visit garden feeders, but in recent years some have learned to nibble at fat balls.

23rd Troops of shaggy inkcap mushrooms can be seen now on grassy roadsides and lawns, and along woodland margins. When they first emerge, the fruit bodies (the mushrooms) of *Coprinus comatus* are elongated, pale eggs covered in soft, peeling suede. They are often clustered in companionable groups, making them noticeable on road verges when you whizz by in a car or on a bike. As they mature, the fleecy-looking caps begin to flare gently outwards, perfectly

illustrating another common name, lawyer's wig. At this stage the edges begin to roll upwards, turn black and dribble an inky fluid (which can apparently be used as actual ink). Within a day or slightly more, the entire cap has deliquesced and all that is left is the stipe (stem) topped with dripping, dark goo. The hyphae, the filaments that make the mycelium or underground network, can exude substances that stun and then digest nematodes, microscopic worms that live in the soil. So, the lawyer's wig has carnivorous tendencies.

24th Ireland's most extensive polders, enclosed for farmland in the nineteenth century, are the Wexford Slobs on either side of the River Slaney estuary. The word 'slob' is from the Irish *slab*, meaning mud or mire. While agriculture is still carried on, two hundred hectares of the north Slob is now occupied by the Wexford Wildfowl Reserve. Over the coming months, tens of thousands of birds will make the reserve their winter quarters. Among them are the Greenland subspecies of the white-fronted goose (the 'white' refers to the snowy patch at the base of the bill). Up to twelve thousand – about half of the world population – of *Anser albifrons flavirostris* arrive from Greenland via Iceland each year, with each leg of the trip taking an arduous eighteen or more hours of flying. The Slobs and the Hebridean island of Islay are the two most important wintering grounds for this goose. Among the many thousands of other birds are internationally important numbers of Bewick's swans and pale-bellied brent geese. The reserve is also a stronghold for the Irish hare as it offers a safe haven with lots of congenial grassland.

25th Larch, that most delicately-branched of conifers, is changing colour. The sombre green of its summer foliage leaches away from the ends of the needles first, revealing underlying yellow and golden pigments. Before dropping its leaves, the whole tree shines with an amber light. The cones stay on the twigs over winter, gradually releasing their winged seeds. Small birds, including redpoll, siskin and crossbills, eat the seeds, as do red squirrels. European larch is a native of the Alps and Carpathians. When it was first introduced to these islands around 1620, it was a sensation, as deciduous conifers were then unknown. One of the oldest and most venerable larches in Ireland is at Killruddery House in County Wicklow – an ancient specimen with pendulous, ground-sweeping limbs, planted in 1750. The well-known walk along the Miners' Road in Glendalough is lined with larch and Scots pine, planted in the mid-nineteenth century. Larch was commonly planted as a 'nurse' species in forestry, to provide shelter for slower-growing broadleaves such as oak and beech and for other conifers, which also helped to brighten their oppressive darkness.

26th The predominant tone of a rural Irish autumn is russet: a colour that favours – among others – foxes, red squirrels and red deer. In recent years perhaps the most prevalent plant contributing to that warm glow is bracken. *Pteridium aquilinum* is our commonest fern, and one of the world's oldest plants: fossil records date back at least fifty-five million years. Originally associated with woodlands, it grew only in the brighter environs of edges and glades. Historically, as woods were cleared bracken was kept in check through grazing and trampling by animals. It was also harvested for bedding, fuel and other purposes. Farming practices have changed, and now that it is no longer controlled, bracken displaces other vegetation in open spaces such as hillsides, neglected farmland and even older dunes. It is a remarkably resilient plant: the underground rhizomes are a metre or two deep and are thus protected from fire. Some stands of bracken are centuries old.

27th The end of October usually sees substantial amounts of fallen leaves mounded up against walls, skittering down pavements and gathering against hedges and tree-roots. Leaf-litter is a biodiverse habitat. Among the more appealing creatures that rely on it are hedgehogs, frogs and bumblebees: all frequently burrow into its dry and rustling depths to create hibernacula for the cold weather. Wrens, dunnocks, blackbirds, thrushes, robins and other birds rummage through the leaves in search of the resident invertebrates. Among these are beetles, spiders, woodlice, millipedes, mites and earthworms. Smaller organisms – some so minute they can be seen only with a microscope – include bacteria, amoebae, rotifers, nematodes, springtails and fungi. These nearly invisible life forms are essential players in the decomposition process. Without them, leaves would not rot and recycle their nutrients into the soil. In the Red Forest near Chernobyl in Ukraine leaves are not decaying properly because microbes, fungi and decomposing insects have not recovered fully after being poisoned by radiation.

28th If you have a shaggy garden, most birds will thank you for it, and the goldfinch more than some. Its natural food is seeds from 'weeds' such as thistle and nettle, and it will also forage among herbaceous perennials that have gone to seed. Plant the biennial teasel, and you will have goldfinches (and teasel) forever. Their chinkling-tinkling calls are unmistakable, as they arrive in groups to winkle out the seeds. Goldfinch numbers in gardens have steadily increased since the 1990s, thanks in part to the surge in feeders offering foods such as nyjer seeds and sunflower hearts. Goldfinches are now among the top ten most frequently recorded garden birds. They hatch two (and occasionally three) well-spaced broods per year, and in some gardens the youngest birds are only now developing their adult plumage. The finishing touches are the perky black-white-and-red head markings.

The colourful feathers and delightful song contributed to the species' depletion during Victorian times and into the twentieth century. Enormous numbers were trapped and sold as caged pets. Dutch artist Carel Fabritius painted a chained goldfinch in 1654. The painting features in Donna Tartt's eponymous novel, *The Goldfinch*.

29th The hawthorn tree has magical powers in Irish folklore, often malevolent. Those who interfered with it did so at their peril, according to the old stories. The perpetrator or their livestock would become ill or paralysed, or be taken away by the fairies. Bringing the blossom indoors was also bad luck. The red berries, however, were less intimidating. The saying, 'When all fruit fails, welcome haw', comes from the west of Ireland. In times of hardship, the bitter and pulpy berries were a lifesaver. Another widespread proverb was: 'A haw year is a *breágh* year' (a fine year). Excavations from Viking Dublin have unearthed haw seeds more than a thousand years old. Old riddles from the west of Ireland often have the haw as their answer. One such collected in County Donegal goes:

As I was going through Barnes Gap
I met a man with a red hat,
A stick in his hand,
A stone in his throat.
Riddle me that and
I'll give you a penny.

A Galway version is: 'A little red soldier on the top of the tree: a stone in his belly and a stick on his back.'

30th Butterfly season is fluttering to an end, with only the occasional battered straggler still on the wing. These late flyers may include species that overwinter here as adults, including peacock, small tortoiseshell and red admiral. The first two regularly hibernate in Ireland, whereas the red admiral has begun to stay for the cold months only in recent years. The comma, once a rarity, but now more frequently seen, has also begun to hibernate here. All the above belong to the vanessid group – our largest and most flamboyant butterflies. They hibernate in a range of places: in sheds, farm buildings and chilly houses, and in crevices in trees, rock faces or walls. The brimstone, our only large yellow butterfly, also hibernates: it usually hides among ivy leaves, which offer the perfect camouflage. Its wings have leaf-like points which allow it to blend in with foliage. Butterflies sometimes wake up and fly about on warm and sunny winter days.

31st Collect blackberries after Hallowe'en at your peril, for the *púca* will be out after dusk spitting or urinating on them, according to folklore. The fairies, sometimes working with that same shape-shifting sprite (variously a goat, horse, bull, pig or indeterminate animal), may likewise be wreaking havoc. They blast fruits, berries and late flowers with their breath – around the time, coincidentally, when the first frosts are hitting. Ragwort or *buachalán* is still in bloom: those who enter a field this evening where it grows may see fairies swinging on it. Its use as a horse for the fairies is well documented. There are stories of hapless people being carried off and waking up in the morning grasping a piece of ragwort. In times past, unfortunate slugs and snails collected on Hallowe'en could foretell the name of one's future spouse. Folklore recorded in Skerries suggested putting a slug onto a plate of flour, where it would write the intended's initials. In County Leitrim, a snail put under the bed would leave a trail spelling out the name. *Oíche Shamhna* was a time for divilment as well as divination. Fern seed collected at midnight conferred invisibility, allowing the bearer to enter houses and rob their contents.

November

1st Autumn storms and high tides toss hefty piles of seaweed onto the upper parts of beaches. Within weeks the soft layers of marine rejectamenta reach a nice stage of decay and provide a habitat for countless organisms. Brown, bristly legged kelp flies lay their eggs among the detritus so that their larvae feed on the bacteria. Sandhoppers, springtails, mites, worms, rove beetles and sea slaters (woodlouse relatives) likewise colonise the ecosystem. These and other invertebrates are food for many birds, and not just seabirds. Pied wagtails, which are equally at home on the paving in towns, take advantage of the bounty, delicately tapping at flies and scuttling abruptly across the surface. Group members maintain contact with staccato calls of 'chitz-ick … chitz-ick!' Occasionally you may see a rock pipit, which belongs to the same family, although it looks more like a miniature thrush, with its brown tones and streaked breast. Stonechats make quick forays to pick up a morsel or two before flitting upwards again to their lookout points on rocks, shrubs or posts.

2nd Beech woods are ablaze now with fluttering golden and peach leaves that turn a warm brown before falling to the ground. This is in contrast to the kilometres of beech hedges edging large properties in the more prosperous parts of the country. Those well-trimmed beech boundaries will remain dressed in this year's dried leaves until next spring. This characteristic, where the leaf shrivels but persists, is known as marcescence. It occurs on immature branches in certain woody species, including beech, hornbeam and some oaks. A hedge is a series of trees kept in perpetual, stunted youth: they are denied by the clippers their right to flower and set seed. The purpose of marcescence is not completely understood and has been much debated. It is possible that the unpalatable withered leaves protect young, vulnerable plants from browsing animals; equally, they may help to preserve next year's buds from winter harm. Another theory is the leaves are timed to fall in spring to provide a moisture-retaining mulch and – as they decompose – nutrients.

3rd Jays, which are woodland birds, are visiting gardens and parks to forage for acorns. Now that trees are losing their leaves, these showy creatures are more visible. Look for medium-sized, mainly pink birds with flashes of white, black and iridescent blue tumbling through the branches. Lone individuals sometimes perch on high, and when they are stationary like this, you can see the trademark Freddie Mercury moustache and the outline of a black-and-white crest, which can be lifted or lowered. The jay is a vocal bird, often heard before seen. The varying calls include a hoarse screech, a 'kraar!', and an imitation of the buzzard's 'mee-ahhh'. Its Latin name, *Garrulus glandarius*, translates roughly as 'the chattering one of the acorns'. The jay was rendered nearly extinct in times past by deforestation and shooting. According to Ussher and Warren's *Birds of Ireland* (1900), it was exterminated in Cork because its wing feathers were used for tying salmon flies.

4th Sea buckthorn is fruiting now along parts of the coast. It bears clusters of beady orange berries that appear glued to the woody stems among willow-like, greyish leaves. The fruits are immensely rich in vitamins C and E, but are difficult to access if you are not a bird. Monstrous, spiny thorns are so well camouflaged that a pierced thigh or hand is inevitable. *Hippophae rhamnoides* is a native of much of northern Europe (including eastern Britain) and parts of

Asia. It was introduced to Ireland in the 1830s or earlier to stabilise dunes and provide shelter. It has now established rather too well in places, including North Bull Island in Dublin. The creeping rhizomes can travel up to two metres per year from the mother plant, creating dense thickets two or three metres tall that shade out almost all other vegetation. If you regularly pass a clump of sea buckthorn on a favourite beach walk, its march is obvious. Nitrogen-fixing nodules on the roots and organic matter from fallen leaves also change the soil composition, making it too rich for species indigenous to coastal habitats.

5 th Although it is November, clouds of dancing midges are airborne on mild days. Not all midge species bite, and of those that do, it is only the females. They need the proteins in fresh blood for egg formation. People who are bitten sometimes wonder what is the point of midges? There is a persuasive answer to this anthropocentric question. Midges of the *Forcipomyia* genus are responsible for pollinating cocoa plants. Therefore, no midges, no chocolate. Closer to home, two midges of this same genus have been recorded pollinating the long, tubular flowers of heather. They have elongated mouthparts that allow them to reach the nectaries in the depths of the flower. Another of the tiny biters, *Serromyia femorata*, resident in Ireland, is worth mentioning for its interesting behaviour. While mating, the female pierces the male's head, releases enzymes that liquefy his innards, and sucks them out. His useless corpse breaks off at his genitalia which then act as a plug to prevent her mating with another male.

6 th Streets and parks are littered with the bristly cases of sweet chestnuts, like herds of miniature green hedgehogs. Also known as the Spanish chestnut, the tree is native to southern Europe and Asia Minor; it has naturalised

throughout much of Europe, including Ireland. The Romans were supposed to have brought it to Britain, but it is unknown when it was first introduced here. According to local tradition, various mature trees were around at the time of the Battle of the Boyne, in 1690. These include one at Oakfield Park in County Donegal and another at Scarva in County Down. King William III was said to have tied his horse to the latter. The rumpled and portly 'Wesley Chestnut' stands in Ashford in County Wicklow. The Methodist founder, John Wesley, was supposed to have preached under it. It was planted in 1718 and is the fattest broadleaf tree in Ireland, with a girth of 10.78 metres. Irish summers are rarely hot enough to swell and ripen sweet chestnuts sufficiently for human consumption, but they feed squirrels, both grey and red. The leaves are the food plant of several moths, while the hollow trunks offer housing for other wildlife.

7th Walk along any river bank, marsh, lake or shallow and rocky coast, and you are likely to see our tallest bird, the grey heron, waiting patiently for its next meal. Standing a metre high, it is equally at home in rural and urban locations. If disturbed, it rises almost vertically, slowly flapping its wings, which have a two-metre span. In flight, the angular curve of its drawn-in neck, its long, spear-like bill and its deeply bowed wings lend it a prehistoric air. In winter, the native population is joined by individuals from Britain and Scandinavia. The grey heron is known vernacularly as the crane, and has much folklore attached to it. A County Meath remedy from the 1930s suggests: 'Crane oil is a good thing for pains. You kill the crane and bury it in a manure heap with his beak in a bottle to catch the oil.' The true crane, which is unrelated, is an occasional visitor to Ireland. It was resident here many centuries ago, according to contemporary reports. Crane bones excavated from archaeological sites have proved its presence.

8 th Earlier in the year, shrubs and trees offered meals of pollen and nectar to flying insects, who delivered spare dustings of pollen from one flower to the next. Unbeknown to themselves, the insects were assisting the plants to have sex, better known as pollination. Now, it is time for the product of those unions, the seeds of the next generation, to be dispersed. Once again, many of the same plants are making bargains with other, mobile species, this time, birds and mammals. Some present juicy bundles of nutrition in the form of fruits, often red or black. Hidden inside the soft flesh are indigestible seeds, which the animals eject at some distance a while after eating. This way the plant ensures that its offspring moves to new pastures with fresh soil and not overshadowed by a parent. Conveniently, the seeds are always deposited with a small packet of organic fertiliser. Our native blackthorn, hawthorn, mountain ash, whitebeam, cherry, crab apple, bramble, viburnum, holly, elder, yew and roses all employ this method. Other plants produce nuts which are cached by birds and small mammals. A number are lost or forgotten and go on to germinate.

9 th Every autumn, about nine thousand wigeon arrive from Iceland, Scandinavia, Finland and Russia to spend the chilly months here. These dabbling ducks, which are considerably smaller than a mallard, are common around the coast and by rivers, lakes and turloughs, especially in the west midlands. They congregate in their hundreds and sometimes thousands: Dublin Bay and the callows around the rivers Shannon and Suck support huge flocks. The round, chestnut-toned heads of the males are conspicuous as they bob up and down while foraging. They are still wearing their breeding plumage, and have a broad, pale stripe on the crown that shines goldenly in some light. Males have a distinctive, clear call: an insistent 'weee-oo … weee-oo', which is far-carrying and evocative. Wigeon can live for a long time and are known

to return regularly to the same wintering grounds. The oldest known individual was ringed at Abberton Reservoir in Essex in 1962. It was shot 3,913 kilometres away in western Siberia in 1996. It was 35 years and 2 months.

10th Winter is just around the corner, but many plants, both wild and cultivated, are still in flower. This is good news for the cumbersome queens of the buff-tailed bumblebee, *Bombus terrestris*, which are abroad all winter. The queens can often be seen nudging the outsides of tubular flowers such as red salvias. Their movements may look blundering and ineffective, but they are intentional. The species has a short tongue, and the necks of some flowers are too long for its reach. The queen is 'nectar-robbing' by piercing a hole at the base of the flower and inserting her proboscis. This means that she has no contact with the anthers or their pollen, and is not fulfilling her part of the expected pollination-for-nectar deal. Up until a couple of decades ago, only the queen survived the chilly season, but in milder areas buff-tailed workers may sometimes be seen, indicating that nests are operating over winter.

11th Around now, overwintering blackcaps are arriving from abroad. These small, dapper birds are unmistakable: the main plumage is a soft beige and grey, with males sporting a neat, jet-black beret and females wearing a matching item in warm, rusty brown. Since the 1990s, the number of this warbler visiting during the cold months has increased greatly, probably as a result of warmer winters. Our winter birds usually arrive from breeding grounds in central Europe while our Irish breeding birds fly farther south to spend the winter in the Mediterranean and north Africa. These little avians weigh no more than twenty grams (five individuals add up to the weight of a standard letter), and migration flights take a toll. Blackcaps are omnivorous in winter, taking insects, bird table food and fruits. Cotoneaster berries are a favourite, as are halved apples. Blackcaps may be small, but they are pugnacious, and will defend a food source against other birds. Numbers in Irish gardens peak in January and February.

12th Ivy is in bloom, pumping out its sweet, musky and slightly iffy fragrance. The flowers are organised into pale-green bobbles bristling with stamens, each topped with a nub of pollen. The inflorescences look like models of atomic structures: pleasingly regular, with highly ordered components. Ivy may be the most important autumn-blooming plant for insects, and a crucial species for their survival. It has plenty of pollen and its easily accessed nectar has a high sugar content, around 49 per cent, according to a University of Sussex study. Examine the flowers closely and you may see white crystals: these are nectar sugars, left behind after water evaporation. The same study showed that honeybees' foraging distances decreased by half during ivy season, which the researchers hypothesise is because of its abundance. Despite its prevalence, ivy's green flowers are often unnoticed by humans. Other insects taking ivy pollen and nectar during this period are hoverflies and other flies, common wasps, bumblebees and the occasional butterfly.

13th The robin is singing, not as noisily as in spring and summer, but the song is just as mellifluous. The rippling, musical warble is interspersed with rapid-fire tick-tick-tick-tick warning calls. Unusually, both sexes sing, and they do so to broadcast their individual territories. Towards the end of December, females enter the domains of prospective mates, and after some half-hearted male posturing, will be accepted. Before cold nights, robins put on more weight, as a buffer against the low temperatures. Research has shown that on mornings when they have retained more body mass overnight, they sing more at dawn. They don't need to feed immediately, and their fat reserves provide enough energy for a proprietorial singing session. In urban areas, robins can sometimes be heard singing at night. Some researchers say that they are beguiled by city lights, while others posit that daytime traffic and other noises cause too much interference, so robins choose the relative quiet of night instead.

14th In mild areas, the tiny coloniser of vintage stone-work, ivy-leaved toadflax, is in flower almost all year. You could pass this Mediterranean import a hundred times without noticing it, so it's worth scanning old walls for the trailing and creeping skeins of fleshy, miniature, ivy-like foliage. The flowers are scaled-down, mauve snapdragons, with whitish, yellow-tinged lips. Stems and leaf-edges are often wine-infused. *Cymbalaria muralis* has been in these islands since the early seventeenth century, its seeds supposedly hitching a ride to Oxford with some marbles from Italy: among its many vernacular names is Oxford weed. Others include coliseum ivy, mother-of-thousands and wandering sailor. It is a plant that associates with humans and is rarely found elsewhere than on walls. The flowers face the sun when they first open, but after they set seed they turn inwards so that the seeds lodge in crevices. One of its fans was the Victorian art critic and painter John Ruskin, who admired it for its exquisite detailing. If ever a plant demanded a magnifying glass, this is it, as it is perfect in all its parts.

15th Wading birds can be tricky to identify, especially in winter light. To the casual birdwatcher, they can merge into an indeterminate 'brown-blob-on-sticks' category as they are usually seen at some distance, when the most obvious feature is their long legs. The lapwing, however, which is one of our most numerous waders – often seen in the hundreds – has an unmistakable silhouette. Both sexes of the pigeon-sized bird have a jaunty backswept crest of wispy feathers, somewhat longer in the male. A member of the plover family, it is also known colloquially as the green plover: while it looks black and white at a distance, its dark feathers have a beautiful green iridescence. In flight, lapwings move with broad and flappy wings, dark on top and with a flash of white underneath. At one time *an pilibín* was caught for food with plaited horsehair snares. Numbers have dwindled, owing to habitat loss and predation by foxes, rats, cats and other birds. The species is on the IUCN (International Union for Conservation of Nature) red list.

16th Many leaves are at their most colourful this month. Some of the best autumnal displays are in grand gardens and large parks, where the diversity of species creates bright splashes on the landscape. Suburban roadsides are also lined with flamboyantly dressed trees. Cherry, rowan and maple are in various stages of leaf fall. In some cases there is as much colour on the ground as on the branches: warm banana, peach, tangerine and plum – all the tones of a well-stocked fruit bowl. Lime and birch have lost nearly all their yellow leaves. Some hazel and oak are still wearing the remnants of their mustard outfits. Willow leaves are yellow too, dangling limply like elongated droplets. Most trees lose their leaves from the highest point first, revealing a tracery of twigs. In the tops of larger trees, the nests of magpies are revealed, dark bundles of sticks. Other birds sometimes use these for shelter over winter, and next year, the magpies may come back and refurbish the nests for re-use.

17th If ever there was a bird to put a person in a good mood, it is the long-tailed tit. Or rather, a troupe of them, because they never travel as singletons. Instead they are a gregarious species, especially in winter when they form familial bands of five to twenty birds, sometimes with other tits in attendance. You hear them before you see them: a spirited and constant call-and-response discourse of 'tseee-tseee-tseee … tseee-tseee-tseee'. Their flight is a series of undulating bursts from tree to tree. There, the little birds tumble acrobatically through the branches, quickly picking off near-invisible insects and spiders with their tiny bills. Their absurdly long tails and petite bodies have conferred on them the nicknames of flying teaspoons and lollipop birds. They don't stay for long in one place, moving on after a few minutes to the next garden or clump of trees. In recent years they have begun to visit feeders, to pick at peanuts or fat balls. At 7–9 grams each, they are our lightest and most cold-vulnerable tit. At night, they gather together in bundles to conserve and share heat. In springtime, the family parties disperse, to avoid interbreeding.

18th Winter heliotrope is starting to flower on banks and roadsides. The tasselled mauve-and-white florets are easy to miss among its great, coarse, round leaves. The Mediterranean native was introduced here in the early nineteenth century, and by 1866 Moore's *Cybele Hibernica* noted it naturalised along roads and hedges in Dublin and Cork. In 1898, Henry Chichester Hart's *Flora of the County Donegal* declared it 'thoroughly established and quite ineradicable in many places'. One of its champions – in multiple editions of his *English Flower Garden* – was the Irish gardener William Robinson. In 1921, although he pronounced it a 'rampant weed … unfit for garden culture', he praised its deliciously fragrant flowers, so useful for winter bouquets. Plant it on 'rough banks and in hedgerows' and allow it to 'carpet a small clump of shrubbery where it may be conveniently gathered'. Alas, his advice and that of others has led to *Petasites fragrans* overpowering our native flora in places. All plants in Ireland are male, which means that they have spread by vegetative means (bits of root or rhizome) rather than by seed.

19th This month often sees an influx of blackbirds into gardens. Females are decidedly brown, with first-year birds still having a few speckles on their bellies. Only fully adult males are entirely jet black, with the species' signature golden bill and eye-rings. Males that hatched this year have browner wings, while their bills vary between black and dirty bronze. Many of these birds are visitors, some from Scotland, and others from Scandinavia and Finland, flying at night-time, to avoid predators. A citizen science project in the UK (involving data from 5,806 observers that was analysed by the British Trust for Ornithology) demonstrated that blackbirds and robins are the first to arrive at garden bird feeders on dark winter mornings. The survey also showed that urban birds rise later than their rural counterparts, even though you could expect the opposite: because built-up areas are brighter, you might think that the higher light levels would encourage earlier feeding. However, cities are warmer, thanks to the 'urban heat island' effect from buildings leaking heat and the hard materials retaining it. Therefore, urban birds expend less energy maintaining body temperature overnight in winter and can refuel later in the morning.

20th The banks of rivers and canals are lined with common reed in its autumn garb, flurries of brushstrokes in russet, beige, ochre and pale green. They are topped with fluffy seedheads that gleam silver in the low sun, but if you bring them indoors for decoration they look disappointingly drab. Waterside willows and alders hold on to some of their leaves, a mix of green and banana yellow. The sword-like leaves of flag iris have collapsed into a messy pile of green and brown. A few flowering stems still stand at awkward angles. The canary-coloured flowers, which were pollinated by bumblebees and flies in summer, are long gone and have been replaced by pods. These have peeled open to reveal six channels of shiny, tan seeds. Each flat seed has a hard coating and an internal air pocket, allowing it to float for over half a year in search of a home, preferably a wet bank. So, an iris that flowered in Celbridge may produce offspring in Chapelizod, seventeen kilometres downriver.

21st November storms pull seaweed from its moorings underwater and fling it into multi-textured, colour-ful piles on beaches – a ragbag of pinks, reds, browns, greens and yellows. Look closely among the tangles and you may find 'mermaids' purses' mixed into the debris. These magical little pods, which look as if they have been moulded from brown or tan rubber, are the egg cases of sharks, skates and ray. Among the most frequent are those of the small-spotted catshark, also known commonly (and confusingly) as the lesser-spotted dogfish. The same size or smaller than your little finger, its cases have coiling tendrils on the ends. The curly appendages help to anchor the containers to seaweeds. Ray and skate egg cases, which may be as large as a hand but are usually much smaller, are more square and have horns at each of the corners. The cases, which contain fertilised eggs and yolks, are deposited by adult females. They offer a secure place for the embryo to develop, a process that can take months.

22nd The leaves on oak trees are falling, but their branches are far from bare. Autumn is the perfect time for admiring the lush plant communities that have settled comfortably onto their outstretched limbs. Mosses, lichens and liverworts gain a foothold in the soggy corrugations of the bark, covering it with a multi-textured blanket. Shamrock-leaved wood sorrel and polypody ferns erupt from the soft green fabric. The evergreen and elegant *Polypodium vulgare* which grows on walls, rocks and dry banks is also an epiphyte, which means it grows on other plants, such as oaks, without harming them. The genus name translates as 'many-footed' and refers to the much-branched rhizome from which the fronds sprout. Vernacular names in Ireland in the past for this common fern included checkle-weed and ladies' comb. During the Victorian fern craze, known as pteridomania, aberrant varieties of native ferns with curiously shaped fronds were eagerly sought out. Patrick Neill Fraser's 1868 *List of British Ferns and their varieties* contains 102 separate variations of the oak polypody.

23rd Ireland has one of the healthiest populations of otters in Europe. There are plenty of them and they are widely distributed throughout the country in watery habitats. Despite their ubiquity, they are difficult to spot as they are wary of humans. Look for them now around dusk and dawn alongside lakes, streams, rivers, canals and along the coast. Their main foods are fish and crustaceans; in bog-land areas, they may have a frog-heavy diet. Otters are sometimes confused with mink, but they are larger – a metre or more – and have a less pointed, more dog-like face, which is reflected in the Irish name *madra uisce* (water dog). Evidence of otters is not difficult to find. They mark territory prominently with spraints, droppings that can be surprisingly sweetly scented. They produce pungent secretions from their anal glands that may act as communication signals to other otters. Look also for footprints, with five toes and claws. In the past otters were valued for medicinal purposes: according to John K'Eogh's *Zoologia Medicinalis Hibernica* of 1739, their pulverised liver was a cure for haemorrhages, powdered testicles were just the thing for epilepsy, otter-skin shoes cured 'pains of the Feet and Sinews' and 'A Cap made thereof helps to cure the Vertigo, and Headach'. Nowadays, otters are a protected species.

24th 'Palm trees' are widespread in coastal counties. Every seaside town has its share of these jolly holiday individuals with their strappy, indestructible leaves. In fact, this tropical-looking tree is unrelated to palms and instead belongs to the same family as asparagus and lily-of-the-valley. *Cordyline australis* is a native of New Zealand and has been planted here since the nineteenth century. In favoured areas, seedlings sprout readily. When the trees are cut down by harsh frost or resentful humans, they often pop up anew. County Wexford is well furnished with cordylines, partly thanks to the Kelly family of Kelly's Hotel near Rosslare, who have presented them to local patrons for decades. Cabbage trees (as they are known) produce highly perfumed panicles of flower in summer, a magnet for bees. The bees' pollinating work is evident now in the huge trusses of thousands of bead-like, cream-coloured fruits. They are high in fats and are a valuable winter food for many birds, including thrushes, starlings, blackcaps and wood pigeons.

25th Ireland's largest duck is the shelduck, a handsome bird sometimes mistaken for a goose, with its long legs and non-waddling gait. The adult plumage is similar on both sexes: dark green head and snowy body with a warm brown chest strap. Males are more boldly marked and have a prominent knob on their wine-red bills. During winter they congregate on the coast, where they swing their bills through wet mud to feed on snails, crustaceans and worms. Our native ducks are joined by migrants from Scandinavia and the Baltic. Large numbers congregate at Strangford Lough in County Down, in Cork Harbour, along the Shannon Estuary and in Dublin Bay. Irish shelducks that have bred in the summer leave their offspring with relatives and go off on an autumn 'migration moult'. They fly either to Bridgwater Bay in Somerset or to the Wadden Sea off northwestern continental Europe. At the latter, they join around two hundred thousand fellow shelducks from Britain, France, Belgium, Holland, Denmark and the Baltic – all renewing their feathers. Irish ducks return between mid-October and spring.

26th The Scots pine is a mighty tree, standing tall on windswept landscapes where it cuts a strong and painterly silhouette against the sky. If you can view it more closely at this time of the year you'll see the rugged, russet-tinged bark and deep green needles lit up by the low winter sun. Some scholars have the pine as the first letter of the Ogham alphabet: *Ailm*. It also represents the second month of the Ogham tree calendar, the winter month, which begins shortly. Until recently it was believed that Ireland's native population of *Pinus sylvestris* had died out between four thousand and two thousand years ago and that all trees were introductions from Scotland from the seventeenth century onwards. However, research by a team at Trinity College Dublin, published in 2016, proved that a tiny outpost of trees in east Clare is part of a community stretching back thousands of years. Analysis of pollen grains preserved in lake sediments revealed the species' continual presence there. The seeds of Scots pines are an important food for our native red squirrels.

27th If you are one of those people who finds themselves sitting by the window and gazing at the birds, then BirdWatch Ireland needs you. The annual Garden Bird Survey, Ireland's longest-running citizen science study, is coming around again shortly. The project, which takes place over thirteen weeks each winter, has been on the go for more than thirty years. It now involves about two thousand households, each of which is engaged in the enjoyable task of counting birds in the garden. The survey is open to everyone with a garden, whether it's a postage stamp or a large parcel of land. It's simple: you record the highest number of each species you see in your garden each week, and either send the results by post at the end of the period or submit them online (details and forms at birdwatchireland. ie). Our gardens are winter sanctuaries for many bird species, and the survey results help BirdWatch monitor how populations are faring. Harsh spells can bring to gardens unexpected and thrilling visitors, such as brambling, snipe and lapwing.

28th The ladybird ranks among everyone's favourite beetles. It is named after 'our lady', the Virgin Mary, who was often depicted wearing a red robe in Christian iconography. In Irish it is *bóin Dé*: God's little cow, a name used also in Spanish and Russian. At present, there are fifteen native species in Ireland, living in parks, gardens, wetlands, grasslands, woodlands, coastal areas and raised bogs. Our most common is the seven-spot, the friend of gardeners, because of its appetite for aphids. The alien harlequin ladybird has arrived in recent years: it has many different spot formations and colours, but is always larger than our natives. Not only does it compete for food with indigenous ladybirds, it also eats them. Ladybirds of all kinds are hibernating now. They gather in leaf litter, on tree trunks, underneath bark, in the top levels of soil, in moss and in dead plant material. Sometimes they come indoors en masse, as they release a pheromone that attracts others of their species. Such gatherings are vulnerable to dehydration and high temperatures. You can *gently* move them into a box with a soft paintbrush and relocate them to a cold shed or greenhouse.

29th Stormy days leave all kinds of debris on forest paths. Among the acorns, chestnuts, beech mast, sticks and leaves, you are likely to find stray chunks of lichen (pronounced either litch-en or like-en: both are correct). There are well over a thousand species in Ireland. The windfalls on the woodland floor may include *Evernia prunastri*, a sage-green lichen, often still attached to its twiggy host. It has a branching form like a tangle of miniature deer antlers, which gives it the common name of stag's horn lichen. Also known as oakmoss, it grows not just on oaks, but on other trees, both deciduous and coniferous, as well as on old fence posts. It can be difficult to identify, as it resembles other woodland species, including several *Ramalina*. But, if you bring home a few samples and let them dry, *Evernia* is unmistakable for its surprisingly sweet, deep, woody fragrance. It has been used in the perfume industry for centuries and was an ingredient in the original Chanel No 5. In Ireland it was used for dyeing wool and was a source of orchil, a pinky-violet dye that appeared after soaking the lichen in urine for some weeks. The colour achieved ranges from a dusty rose to a shocking pink, a surprisingly artificial-looking pigment to arise from a sedately toned lichen.

30th Although it is the last day of November, there are still dozens of plants in flower, especially in urban areas where buildings and paving keep temperatures a few degrees warmer. Some of the species are introductions from the Mediterranean and other arid, stony places. Over the years they have escaped from gardens and have set up homes in cracks in pavements and masonry and on waste ground. These nutrient-poor, stony habitats are reminiscent of their native soil. One of the showiest is the snapdragon, originally from southwest Europe and the Mediterranean. The flowers on naturalised plants may be yellow or salmon, but they are mostly bright pink with a splash of yellow on the lips. The species has been living in walls in Ireland since at least the beginning of the nineteenth century. The related purple toadflax and ivy-leaved toadflax are also in flower, as is red valerian. Natives still blooming include yarrow, dead-nettles, sow-thistles, herb Robert and groundsel, with its tiny Bart Simpson heads. Gorse is in flower, as it is every month of the year, which gives us the saying 'when the gorse is out of bloom, kissing's out of fashion'.

December

1 **st** The hawfinch is rare, but worth looking out for between mid-autumn and early spring. This visitor from central Europe looks like a chunky and warm-toned chaffinch, with a huge head and a massive bill. In *The Natural History of the Birds of Ireland* (1853) John J. Watters notes with the typical human-centred judgement of the time that it is 'one of those birds without the slightest pretensions to beauty or elegance of form, owing to the immense disproportion between the size of the head and body'. Its immense bill, he goes on to note, makes it of very little value as a caged bird. True to its name, it eats haws, seeds and all, but it is also attracted to the seeds of hornbeams and other trees. Birds turn up most years at Curraghchase Forest Park in County Limerick, where many hornbeams were planted in the nineteenth century. It can be difficult to spot, as it spends most of its time up in the tree canopy, feeding. The hawfinch's remarkably large head contains robust muscles that power its hefty bill, allowing it to chomp through hard nuts and kernels, including cherry stones.

2 **nd** To us land-dwellers, seaweed can seem like an amorphous bundle of slippery matter when we come across it on beach walks. Yet, we have at least five hundred species growing around our coast. This exceptional diversity is probably because Ireland is at the farthest limit both for warm-water and cold-water species. Among the most common are egg wrack (*Ascophyllum nodosum*) and bladder wrack (*Fucus vesiculosus*), species that live in the intertidal zone, where they are alternately submerged and uncovered as the water ebbs and flows. Both have balloons of air incorporated into their structure. These act as flotation devices, lifting the plants upwards when the tide is in so that they can photosynthesise. The sacs on egg wrack – as the name suggests – are oval, distinct and beadlike. The plant produces one large air sac per year on each frond, so you can age the fronds that you find. The sacs on bladder wrack look more like blisters and may be round or slightly irregular. They are often in small groups, like tiny sections of bubble wrap.

3rd It is the start of the noisy season for foxes. As the mating season gets under way their eerie calls can be heard more frequently at night. Vocalisations include a long, howling 'e-wowwww!' and a hoarse, rasping, high-pitched horror-movie shriek. The latter is often referred to as the vixen's scream, but both sexes are known to utter it. Cubs born earlier are now fine-looking animals with thick coats and luxuriant tails: they will never look better in their lives. Young males are more mobile than their sisters and will attempt to muscle into the domains of older foxes. This is a dangerous undertaking: death is more likely in an unfamiliar environment and traffic accidents claim many lives. Young females have a higher survival rate. Those that remain in their mother's territories become subservient to the dominant vixen. A fox's lifespan can be short: a study in Northern Ireland showed that 40 per cent die before the end of their first year. Only a quarter may live to be two years old and a tiny percentage last longer than five years.

4th Now that trees have shed their leaves, it is easier to see the birds among their branches. The mistle thrush often perches in the tops of tall trees in open woodland, parks and large gardens. It is larger and more upright than the song thrush and cooler in its plumage. At a distance, it can appear almost silvery among the dark tracery of branches. When it flies, its white underwings and outer tail feathers are visible.

It often takes off while uttering a fast-paced and high-pitched rattle. Wing-beats are stiff and mechanical, and interspersed with short glides. It takes its name from mistletoe, a favourite plant, although here it is more likely to eat berries such as holly. An individual bird will guard a tree jealously, chasing off all comers. Mistle thrushes begin to sing next month, performing even in inclement weather, which gives them the vernacular name of storm-cocks. The song is not unlike that of a blackbird, but with a more hesitant and mournful character.

5th Crab apples are still clinging to the branches of trees along streets and in gardens. Many of the more modern varieties have been selected by breeders because they are unpopular with birds, which seems mean-spirited. The spring flowers, however, provide welcome food for insects. The true wild crab apple (*Malus sylvestris*) is a rare thing in Ireland, and it can be difficult to positively identify. Species cross readily, so native crabs and domestic apples can produce all kinds of mongrel offspring. The wild-looking apples that we find growing in hedgerows are likely to be such crosses or seedlings of domesticated varieties. In Brehon law, the apple is one of the seven *airig fedo*, the 'nobles of the wood'. Its fruit was valuable, the wood was fine-grained and resilient, and the bark was used in dyeing and tanning. *Úll* and *úllghort*, the words for apple and orchard, occur in many Irish place names, including Oulart in County Wexford and Ballynahoulort in County Kerry.

6th Winter brings skeins of wild geese flying purposefully overhead, accompanied by clamorous honking, cron-king and yelping as the birds maintain contact with each other. At this time of the year, six main species of geese can be seen in Ireland. All are substantial birds: lumbering and flat-footed on the ground, serene on the water and overwhelmingly graceful in flight. The six can be conveniently divided into three 'grey' and three 'black-and-white' species. The former include pink-footed (from Greenland and Iceland), white-fronted (Greenland) and greylag. Some of these last have come from Iceland, but many are feral birds, escaped from domesticity. Among the black-and-white kinds is the barnacle goose from Greenland, with its distinctive white face, like a Venetian carnival mask. The Canada goose is another: most that we see are year-round residents, absconders from wildfowl collections. Some, however, have come from abroad, travelling with white-fronted or barnacle geese. The last of the black-and-whites are the light-bellied brent geese from the Canadian Arctic. These are the geese that you are most likely to see around Dublin Bay.

7th   Often, plants that bloom in the colder months have powerful, far-reaching fragrances. Examples include wintersweet and Christmas box, headily scented, woody plants that are familiar to gardeners. In winter, pollinators are scarce, so plants hoping to reproduce now must broadcast their scented advertisements as widely as possible. In Ireland, the species with the strongest winter perfumes are non-native, and as the insects that they are designed to attract are often not present, their scented signalling may go unanswered. Two exceptions among the exotics are daphne, which has tiny tubular flowers of pink or white; and mahonia, with bright yellow, tight and beady flowers. Both are well visited by the winter-flying, buff-tailed bumblebee (*Bombus terrestris*). Mahonia is especially useful: each plant has hundreds of flowers supplying both nectar and pollen, and research has shown that the individual flowers have higher nectar volumes than most species. Bumblebees conserve valuable energy when mahonia is available, and their nests are more likely to thrive.

8th   Little egrets are a common sight, fishing on the edges of wetlands and other watery places. In the dim

December light, their snowy plumage and rapier-like black bills stand out against the muted and muddy tones of winter nature. About two-thirds the size of the grey heron, these elegant birds were once scarce. They were seen only occasionally, rare vagrants that pitched up in Ireland from southern Europe. They first bred here in 1997 when twelve pairs nested in a heronry along the River Blackwater in Cork, just a year after the species reproduced successfully at Poole Harbour in Dorset. They established quickly: the most up-to-date data (from the winter of 2015/16) gives the all-Ireland population as 1,390 birds. The little egret has increased its range in Britain and Ireland faster than any other bird in decades. Since 1994, the Irish winter population has grown by a staggering 3747.2 per cent. The greatest increases were early during this period, as the species filled unoccupied habitat niches. Irish birds are not static and can range great distances: individuals hatched in Galway were subsequently spotted in the Azores and Iceland. Little egrets were once hunted for their long and wispy breeding plumes, much in demand by milliners.

9th Trees are bare and their skeletal forms are clearly visible. Keep an eye out for 'witches' brooms' in birch trees, dense bundles of twiggy growth that look like nests built by manic magpies. They are caused by a parasitic fungus, *Taphrina betulina*. It infects buds and young shoots, making the tips multiply and produce a proliferation of spindly shoots. In time, the 'brooms' can reach a great size. Some trees have multiple growths that look like dark smudges on the tracery of branches. They are a kind of gall, where an organism invades a plant, modifies its structure and uses the resulting material for food and shelter. In this case, the parasite is a fungus, but galls are also caused by bacteria, nematodes, mites and insects. Only young cells can be made to produce galls, as they are compliant and versatile. They are able to mutate into whatever tissue the galling agent dictates: brooms, lumps, bristles, bumps, orbs and other swellings. Witches' brooms are harmless and do not affect the tree's vigour.

10th Woodlice are a much-maligned group, yet they are among nature's great decomposers. They feed primarily on decaying plant matter and do the natural world a favour by getting rid of its rubbish. Unusually for land-based invertebrates, they are crustaceans and are related to lobsters, shrimp and barnacles. They are always found in dampish areas such as under logs, in compost heaps and in cellars. The woodlouse has more vernacular names than possibly any other creepy-crawly: in Ireland alone, it is a slater, clock, pig and penny pig. In Britain, dozens of names have been recorded, including bibble bug, chizzle ball and tiddy hog. The scientific name for a common genus is *Porcellio*, which comes from the Latin for 'little pig', *porcellus*. To the woodlouse spider, however, it is just dinner. This unmistakable arachnid has a beige abdomen and rust-coloured thorax and legs. It was unintentionally introduced from the Mediterranean during the nineteenth century. It hunts woodlice at night.

11th Incongruous plants of pampas grass, that front-garden stalwart, may surprise walkers in certain areas, especially along the east and southeast coast. It has made its home in the wild in counties Wexford, Waterford and Dublin, hoisting up its fluffy, silvery seedheads on cliff sides and wastelands. In the past ten years, the grass has been popping up more frequently in Ireland, originally from carelessly dumped garden plants, and more recently from seed. Commuters travelling on the Dart in south Dublin can see it adorning the manmade islands in Booterstown's bird sanctuary. The native territory of *Cortaderia selloana* is across wide swathes of South America: in Brazil, Argentina, Chile and Uruguay. The species has a unique connection with Ireland. In

1842 the botanic garden in Glasnevin was the first place in the world outside its native range where the grass germinated and flowered. The seeds had been sent by Scotsman John Tweedie, who emigrated to South America in the mid-1820s. From Dublin, plants were introduced to the rest of Europe.

12th If you spend any time on the road in County Wicklow or north County Dublin, you're likely to see a red kite or two above, gliding gracefully with angled, black-tipped, white-marked wings and forked tail. The body, inner wings and tail are fox-toned, making this large raptor easily identifiable. It often circles slowly over roadways, watching for small prey below, such as mice and rats. It also feeds on roadkill: carrion is an important component in its diet, more so in winter than in other seasons. All Ireland's red kites are birds that have been introduced from Wales – or their offspring. The species was wiped out at the end of the eighteenth century, through habitat loss and hunting. Large birds of prey were ruthlessly persecuted, as they were wrongly seen as a threat to livestock and game birds. The species was reintroduced by the Golden Eagle Trust, in association with the National Parks and Wildlife Service and the Welsh Kite

Trust. Between 2007 and 2011, 158 birds were released in County Wicklow and north County Dublin. The first Irish chicks were raised in 2010.

13th Now is the season for finding gangs of snails gathered in disused plant pots, in crevices in walls, holes in trees and other sheltered places. During winter, the brown garden snail retreats into hibernation to prevent frost damage to its water-abundant body. It seals over its mantle collar (the exposed tissue at the shell opening) with hardened mucus to reduce dehydration during the quiescent period. James Ward, an English philosopher and psychologist with an abiding interest in nature, described in 1897 an experiment he conducted with a pair of snails. After they had copulated, he placed them into 'a closed pot of earth', where they 'soon sealed themselves up'. Ten-and-a-half months later, one had died, while the other had shrunk to a third its former bulk. After 'being moistened and supplied with food, [it] soon began to eat and to thrive'. Within two months, it regained its volume, burrowed into the ground and laid a clutch of eggs. These duly hatched into 'a little colony of vigorous young snails'.

14th Fungi are still pushing up through woodland floors and decaying wood. The mushrooms that we see are tiny parts of a much larger life form: they are the tip of a fungal iceberg. The main body is the mycelium, an unseen network of microscopic feeding threads snaking through the soil or wood. The mushrooms or toadstools are the fruiting bodies: their job is to manufacture and disperse spores so that the great organism underneath can colonise other areas. In fruit bodies with gills (such as field mushrooms), the gills are absolutely plumb-line vertical. Spores are ejected horizontally from the gill walls and immediately meet enough air resistance to change course and plummet downwards. Therefore, no spore crashes wastefully into the opposite wall.

The aerodynamics at the base of the cap further aid successful dispersal. A band of relative stillness for the first couple of millimetres prevents spores being blown back into the gills. After the quiet zone, turbulence coming off the cap picks up the spores and carries them off into the world. Nature is a sophisticated engineer.

15th 'When the Blackbird sings before Christmas, she will cry before Candlemas' was a County Meath saying, according to the Reverend Charles Swainson in his *Provincial Names and Folklore of British Birds* (1885). Female blackbirds don't sing, but perhaps this means that if she gets frisky and goes into breeding mode too soon, she'll not be successful. Our native blackbirds are joined in winter by visitors from abroad, making blackbirds the second most commonly seen garden bird in this season. Occasionally, individuals with patches of white plumage turn up. These leucistic birds have a genetic mutation that inhibits pigment from reaching the feathers. Blackbirds were not appreciated by those with thatched cottages, for they were among the birds that stripped off the material while looking for food. In his autobiographical novel, *The Green Fool*, Patrick Kavanagh remembers blackbirds searching 'for the little red worms in the decayed straw'. Sometimes 'spitting rain would startle the sleeping faces of the children in their beds, and indeed I often heard father tell of a wet night when he had to hold an umbrella over himself and my mother in their bed'.

16th The Norway spruce used to be the traditional Christmas tree species, but it has since been overtaken by Nordmann and noble firs. None are native to Ireland, but conifers are familiar in our landscape. Conifer plantations can be lifeless and dark, with a marked absence of a shrubby under-layer. But clearings, trails and the margins can support a range of mammals and birds. Among the former are pine marten, red squirrel and bats. The long-eared owl nests and hunts in conifers, while treecreeper, siskin, goldcrest and coal tit are among the few songbirds that readily frequent them. The last three happily decamp to gardens when food becomes scarce, at the end of winter or in harsh weather. Coal tits also live and breed in gardens, and are a familiar sight all year. They are tiny, top-heavy birds, with heads that seem too small for their dainty bodies. The head is black with pale cheeks and a distinctive, vertical white stripe on the nape. Ireland has a unique subspecies of coal tit (*Parus ater hibernicus*), with warm, yellow-ish cheek patches.

17th A nyjer seed feeder in a garden is guaranteed to bring in flocks of goldfinches. Fill it and they will find it. Sometimes they are accompanied by linnets, little brown finches that have become more frequent garden visitors in recent years. During winter, linnets are almost completely brown, and from a distance could be mistaken for sparrows. Closer inspection reveals white-edged wing and tail feathers, and tweedy chests, neatly streaked in buff and brown. Their behaviour at a feeder is calmer and less 'cheeky' than sparrows. Often, before dropping down to a garden, they perch in a nearby tree, evenly spread through the upper branches, like ornaments on a well-dressed festive tree. During the breeding season, male linnets acquire red patches on the crown and bib, similar to those of lesser redpolls. Linnets, however, are a heavier and less acrobatic bird: they always feed upright and never dangle, as redpolls do. Linnets that are around now may be residents or winter visitors.

18th Kelp is plentiful on beaches, torn from its footings by powerful, storm-driven waves. These brown seaweeds grow mostly in the low shore area, on rocks that are exposed only at the lowest of tides. We have five indigenous kelps, including three that commonly wash up. Both oarweed

(*Laminaria digitata*) and strapweed (*L. hyperborea*) have a thick stem, known as a stipe, and a great, flattened hand of a frond. Oarweed is smoother and its stipe is flexible, whereas that of strapweed is more brittle. Sugar kelp forms long, ruffled and crinkled ribbons, up to three metres long. Kelps are attached to rocks with a 'holdfast', a structure that looks like a bundle of roots. But, as seaweeds derive all their nutrition from the water, the holdfast serves only as an anchor. Look for patches of pale, fine mesh on oarweed and strapweed, like fragments of thin net curtain bonded to the surface. These lacy growths are sea mats: colonies of tiny animals known as zooids that live together and operate as a single organism, a bryozoan. Take a photo with your phone and zoom in on it, or bring a piece home and look at it with a magnifier. Each creature is contained in a neat, rectangular exoskeleton, and thousands are joined together in a mat.

19th Why are there no black-headed gulls around at this time of year? Habitual walkers along Ireland's piers, promenades and lakesides might be idly wondering about this phenomenon. Indeed, the small gull, one of Ireland's most numerous, is still with us, often accompanied by visitors from northern and eastern Europe. However, it is not wearing its characteristic dark hood. The whole-face mask – which is actually deep-brown rather than black – appears only during the breeding season. It develops in mature birds from early springtime and is often gone again by late summer. Non-breeding birds, which are all about us, have a white head with a sooty splotch behind the eye and a slight grey shadow on the forehead. They have distinctive red legs and slender red bills. One of the old vernacular names in Ireland was the red-shank gull. Black-headed gulls are widespread inland as well as along coasts. The second part of the Latin moniker, *Larus ridibundus*, means laughing. It pays tribute to the gull's high-pitched, overwrought vocalisations.

20th Ivy is always a sterling plant for wildlife, but especially during the colder months, when it becomes like a busy hotel sheltering and catering for many creatures. The black berries that ripen in winter and spring are a high-fat food for birds, among them thrushes, blackbirds, blackcaps, wood pigeons and collared doves. Smaller birds such as tits, wrens and goldcrests take shelter among the thick, waterproof leaves. They search too for hibernating insects on which to dine. Among those hiding in ivy in this season are the marmalade hoverfly and the holly blue butterfly (the second generation of which hibernates in pupal form). The pupae of the yellow-barred brindle moth may also be secreted in its dry depths. Caterpillars of the swallow-tailed moth take on the guise of a dead twig and are almost impossible to spot. Ivy is laden with folklore: the evergreen leaves represent fertility and life, while its ability to cling symbolises fidelity. In parts of Ireland, it was thought unlucky to bring ivy indoors, except at Christmas time. Mad Sweeney, the king who took to the wilds after being cursed, was said to roost alone up in the ivy.

21st The winter solstice, the day with the fewest hours of light and the longest night, almost always falls on the 21st or 22nd of this month. In pagan times, bonfires were lit on the evening of the solstice: to encourage the sun to return, it is said. The tradition of the Christmas log, or *Bloc na Nollaig*, may have stemmed from this. The log was lit on Christmas Eve, instead of during the solstice. It was placed at the back of the fireplace and kept burning for many hours, bringing abundance and luck to the household. In Ireland, the log was sometimes bog deal (pine wood that had been preserved in the bog), or more often, oak. The log was supposed to be given to the household or harvested from one's own land. A small bit of unburnt wood was sometimes kept back until the following year when it was used to ignite the new log and thus pass the fire from one year to the next.

22nd The robin is the most frequently seen bird in Irish gardens, according to BirdWatch Ireland's annual garden bird survey. At this time of the year, its image is omnipresent indoors also. Since Victorian times, robins have featured on Christmas cards. They were shown delivering letters, like miniature British postmen, who then wore scarlet tunics and were known as 'robins' or 'redbreasts'. In Ireland, there were many myths about *an spideog*. One says that his red breast is a result of scorching himself while fanning a fire to warm the baby Jesus in the stable at Bethlehem. Whatever the folklore, the little bird has a long association with humans, especially gardeners and those who work outdoors. Robins evolved alongside woodland creatures such as wild boar which disturb the soil with snout and hoof, exposing worms, larvae and other nutritious tidbits. To a robin, a gardener is just another animal rootling around in the soil.

23rd Holly is in bright red berry, providing food for plenty of bird species. The dense, spiky foliage offers a safe roosting place. Male and female flowers are borne on separate plants, so reproduction depends entirely on insects ferrying pollen from plant to plant in early summer. Holly is tough and adaptable, growing in habitats as varied as woodland, heathland and on the sides of mountains. In the Burren's limestone paving, holly stretches up from the fissures (the grykes) only to be clipped into bonsai trees by wind and livestock. The Irish, *cuileann*, has given us many place names, including Glencullen and Kilcullen. In Brehon law, holly was a noble of the wood; in folklore, it was a 'gentle' bush, belonging to the fairies. Cut it down and your hair might fall out, your cow become ill, or sudden insanity or storms strike your house. The spines of the leaves were said to act as lightning conductors. Those same spines lend their sharpness to the second part of the botanical name, *Ilex aquifolium*. The 'aqui' may come from the Latin 'aquila' for eagle (with its sharp talons) or from 'acus', meaning needle. Either way, the leaves are unforgettably prickly.

24th

'Twas the night before Christmas, when all through the house
Not a creature was stirring, not even a mouse

… As it happens, on this most quiet of nights, mice could well be chattering their heads off, while remaining entirely unheard by humans. Most of what *Mus musculus* says remains inaudible to our insensitive ears. This is because mice communicate mainly in the ultrasonic range (frequencies greater than 20 kilohertz). Any squeals or peeps that we detect under a cupboard or floorboard are the rodent's bass notes. Ultrasound detectors have shown that mice 'sing': they produce complex vocalisations featuring 'syllables' in a variety of volumes, durations and frequencies, sometimes using repeated phrases. Male mice sing to potential mates during courtship chases; if the female is receptive, she sings also, and slows her pace. An uninterested female, on the other hand, remains silent and does not slacken. Male mice are keen singers and will start vocalising when presented with the scent of a female. Mouse voices can range across five octaves, a feat achieved by only a few human singers, including Axl Rose of Guns N' Roses and Mariah Carey.

25th Mistletoe is an introduced plant in Ireland, although it is native in Britain. It is a hemiparasitic species, growing on and taking most of its nutrients from apple, lime, hawthorn, poplar, maple and willow, among other trees. It is often associated with oak, but there are no records of oak hosting it in Ireland. Mistletoe has been recorded at seventy-five locations, with the greatest population at Glasnevin's National Botanic Gardens. In the 1840s, curator David Moore received seeds of *Viscum album* from Dr Richard Whately, Archbishop of Dublin. He managed to establish it on half a dozen trees. It can still be seen in the gardens. The plant gives its name to the mistle thrush. The seeds are dispersed by birds, often when they are excreted. The most efficient distributor of the seeds, however, is the blackcap. It swallows only the skin and pulp and wipes each seed off its beak onto a branch, where it sticks firmly, aided by the berry's glue-like tissue. This is more effective than hit-and-miss bird droppings.

26th The wren may be one of Ireland's tiniest birds, but it is also one of the loudest. Its song can cut through the powerful soundscapes of spring dawn chorus or morning traffic. Relative to its size, it vocalises at ten times the volume of a crowing rooster. When it is not announcing its presence in song, the wren is scuttling through ivy and undergrowth looking for spiders and insects. In cold weather, it must eat up to 40 per cent of its body weight daily to survive. On winter nights, wrens often roost communally in crevices or bird boxes. The roosts are managed by a male wren, who invites others of both sexes to join him. As spring approaches, however, he excludes other males and admits only females. *An dreolín* is safe today from the old Saint Stephen's Day tradition of 'hunting the wren'. But, in times past, the 'wren boys' procession included a real wren, killed and hung from a holly bush or the like. The wren is the king of the birds, according to myth, because it was able to fly the highest. Sneakily, it gained the necessary altitude by hitching a lift on the back of an eagle.

27th It is possible that the wren's mythological chauffeur was the golden eagle, one of our two native eagles. In common with other large Irish raptors, the species was rendered extinct here through persecution, in this case around 1912. Later, between 1953 and 1960, a single pair bred on a County Antrim sea cliff, but after that sightings were sparse. The Antrim eagles fed mainly on rabbits and hares. Debris recovered from plucking sites and the nest showed that the hares were of the short-legged Scottish race, a subspecies not found in Ireland. The birds, therefore, were nipping across the North Channel to hunt. Golden eagles were reintroduced to County Donegal in a programme that started in 2001, using young eagles from the Scottish Highlands. Over the following years, 61 birds were released. The first chick fledged successfully in 2007 and in

2018, one of the Donegal-bred birds reared its own chick. About twenty chicks have since fledged. In the coming weeks, pairs may be displaying over their territories: look for them in Glenveagh, Inishowen Peninsula, the Bluestack Mountains and the Glencolumbkille Peninsula.

28th The low light at this time of the year and the lack of distracting foliage make tree trunks stand out starkly. Birch, with its pale bark, is most noticeable. The gleamingly white trees of front gardens are varieties of Himalayan birch (*Betula utilis*). Why so white? One reason is that the light bark reflects heat rather than absorbing it. In very cold regions, rapid heating and cooling can be injurious to the tree, so a reflective bark prevents extreme and abrupt changes in temperature. In the 1880s, seed of a birch that develops a very chalky bark when young was collected in the Himalayas by plant-hunter Joseph Hooker. It was grown at the botanic gardens belonging to Trinity College in Dublin. The variety is named 'Trinity College'. Our two native birches are not as ghostly-looking, perhaps because our climate is more clement. Downy birch (*B. pubescens*) and silver birch (*B. pendula*) are hard to tell apart, and the two may cross, causing more confusion. Birches are pioneer species, being among the first to colonise bogs and other marginal land. Their seeds are eaten by redpolls and small finches.

29th Some people don't like starlings: they are noisy birds with a range of wittering, snickering and squeaky-wheel calls that can irritate rather than enchant. A small gang can polish the food off a bird table in minutes. But these rapacious yobbos – with their shiny, spotty suits and sharp, questing bills – are the performers of one of the most gracefully choreographed displays in nature. During winter, our starling population is swelled by a huge surge of birds from the continent, and they come together in their thousands to form pre-roosting flocks at dusk. Birds arrive from as far as thirty kilometres to join the murmuration, as it is called. Before settling down for the night in reedbeds, woodland or even under a bridge, the flock performs a magnificent sky dance: gliding, dipping and soaring as if they are a single organism. They move with calligraphic ease and precision, racing into dark ribbons and super-accelerated swirls of ink in the sky. The purpose of the manoeuvre is unclear, but may be to confound predators or exchange information. Locations with regular murmurations include Albert Bridge in Belfast, Lough Ennell in County Westmeath, Cahore Marsh in County Wexford and Wicklow town.

30th Ash is one of the easiest trees to identify at a distance in winter. Mature specimens are often loftier than other trees, a fact reflected in the second part of the Latin name, *Fraxinus excelsior*, which translates as 'higher'. Ash is sparsely branched, with the lower branches hanging downwards in a pleasingly gothic manner. The most obvious definers are the bunches of brown 'keys' that dangle messily from the twigs well into spring, and which are eaten by various finches. Squirrels – both the native red and the introduced grey – also eat them. Close-up, ash twigs are smooth and grey; each has a terminal bud of matte black, while the subordinate buds are arranged in neat pairs. In Irish folklore, ash has magical powers, both good and evil. After hawthorn, it is the most frequent tree at holy wells. Foraging websites offer recipes for pickling unripe ash keys, which must then be matured for three months before eating. There is scant information on their flavour.

31st Ferns, according to folklore collected in County Carlow, are lucky plants. There was a custom for farmers to gather them on New Year's Eve from every field on the farm and to bring them home. They were put into a little bag and hung behind the door for 'the round of the year'. In Slovenia, fern seed (spores) could be caught on a white cloth and put under the animals' bedding in the stable on this night. The spores conferred on humans the ability to hear the animals' conversations during the dark hours. These might include predictions for the coming year concerning their owner's fate and their own. In Ireland, animals were also supposed to speak, but on Christmas night. New Year's Eve is also a time for seeing one's future spouse in one's dreams. Holly and ivy leaves are put under the pillow and this verse recited:

Oh ivy green and holly red,
Tell me, tell me whom I shall wed.

While for many of us this day is significant and symbolic, the natural world feels no such weightiness. Instead, it is just a day like any other, a small moment in the enduring cycle of death and renewal. Life goes on.

Acknowledgements

I owe buckets of gratitude to the many people who helped me with this book. Firstly, to Richie Oakley, who was my editor at both *The Sunday Times* and *The Times Ireland*; he introduced me to HarperCollins in Dublin, then being steered by Eoin McHugh, to whom I am also grateful.

At HarperCollins and William Collins, a clever and committed crew of people has seen this book through from start to finish: in Dublin, Nora Mahony has been an attentive and kind editor, while in London, Myles Archibald and Hazel Eriksson shepherded along the many elements that end up making a fully-formed book. Copy editor Sally Partington weeded out clangers and howlers with precision and sensitivity and made many useful suggestions. I am grateful also to the publicity and sales teams, Patricia McVeigh, Ciara Swift, Tony Purdue and Jacq Murphy, and to Ben Hurd and Ammara Isa in London. Thank you to Chris Wright in production, typesetter Jacqui Caulton, proofreader Rachel Malig and indexer Ben Murphy.

Thank you to Robert Vaughan for producing such beautiful and characterful illustrations. It was such a treat to see them piling up one by one, a treasury of Irish flora and fauna.

I'm tremendously grateful to Linda Daly and Frank Fitzgibbon, my editors at *The Sunday Times*, for giving my nature column such a congenial home. Thanks also to Niall Toner, Eileen Martin, Dara Flynn and the other kind souls at that paper.

I am indebted to Eric Dempsey, birdman extraordinaire, for taking time to carefully read all the bird entries and to offer valuable suggestions. Niall Hatch and Brian Burke of

BirdWatch Ireland also offered lavish help with many queries, as did Ferdia Marnell of the National Parks and Wildlife Service. I am grateful to the friends and fellow nature-lovers on Twitter who generously answered queries and helped with IDs. Thank you also to the following, who were supportive in different ways: Catriona Brennan, Juanita Browne, Helen Crowley, Rob and Valerie Dalton, Andrew Davidson, Séamus de Pouvier, Liz Devlin, Roy Dooney, Morna Ferguson, Paul Gaster, Katy Hayes, Greta Hickey, Matthew Jebb, Pam Joyce, Feargus McGarvey, Sara Macken, Allan Mee, Frank Miller, Richard Murphy, Lorcan O Toole, Ena Prosser, Brendan Sayers, Judith Spring, Jonny Taylor, Paddy Tobin, and my nature-loving friends at Danesmoate.

Finally, thank you to my family and almost family, especially my good friend Mary Davies, my sister Katherine A. Powers and my niece Emily Farl Powers – who variously listened to, advised and shoved me along. I am forever grateful to my husband, Jonathan Hession, who has sustained, encouraged and cheered me through every single word of this book. My late brother, Hugh, brought me on many nature-watching excursions when I was still a teenager. He showed me various birds and plants, introduced me to different plant families and to the unexpected joys of botanical Latin. This book is dedicated to him.

Endnotes

i   Some of the folklore quoted throughout can be found in the National Folklore Collection, housed at University College, Dublin. It can be accessed online at duchas.ie

ii The Brehon Laws were an ancient system of legislation dating back to pre-Christian times and operating in some form until the seventeenth century.

iii The vernacular sun-fish (basking shark) should not be confused with the actual sunfish (*Mola mola*), another ocean-going giant occasionally spotted in northern European coastal waters, including off the west and southwest of Ireland.

iv The 'doctrine of signatures' is a medical system dating back to the Ancient Greeks that still survives in extreme corners of herbalism in the present day. It is based on the faulty premise that plants resembling parts of the body can be used to treat ailments in those same parts.

Resources

Websites

batconservationireland.org information on Ireland's nine bat species, details of events and bat groups.

biodiversityireland.ie the National Biodiversity Data Centre collects and manages data on Ireland's biological diversity; website includes citizen science areas for entering your own sightings and viewing collected data; information on species and diversity initiatives.

birdwatchireland.ie everything to do with Ireland's birds: help with identification; news, events, advocacy, research, details of nature reserves and places to see birds; publications; shop.

bsbi.org Botanical Society of Britain and Ireland: resources for botanists and enthusiasts, including plant distribution maps, advice on recording plants, annual New Year Plant Hunt.

buglife.org.uk organisation devoted to 'saving the small things that run the planet' including insects, worms, woodlice, spiders and some marine invertebrates.

bumblebeeconservation.org.uk bumblebee information and advice: identification, gardening, land management, learning zone for children.

butterflyconservation.ie butterfly reports and news from around Ireland.

butterfly-conservation.org treasury of information on British and Northern Irish butterflies and moths.

butterflyireland.com and **irishbutterflies.com** two basic but efficacious websites providing information on Ireland's butterflies.

ipcc.ie Irish Peatland Conservation Council: information on bog habitats and species.

irelandswildlife.com wildlife news and tours, species profiles, articles.

irishbirding.com sightings of rare and unusual birds, regularly updated.

irishlichens.ie lichens of Ireland with photos and descriptions by Jenny Seawright.

irishmoths.net moths of Ireland with photos and descriptions by Jenny Seawright.

irishwildflowers.ie photographs and details of over 800 native and introduced Irish wildflowers; includes links to Irish trees, ferns, grasses, rushes, sedges, mosses and liverworts; all by Jenny Seawright.

irishwildlifematters.ie information on Irish wildlife rescue and first aid.

iwdg.ie Irish Whale and Dolphin Group website with species descriptions, news, events; pages for reporting strandings and sightings.

iwt.ie Irish Wildlife Trust website, dedicated to conserving wildlife and its habitats.

mothsireland.com basic but information-packed website on Irish moths, includes sections on common moths, day-flying moths, caterpillars; thousands of photos.

nativewoodlandtrust.ie charity devoted to conserving and replanting Ireland's native woodlands, details of woodlands to visit.

npws.ie National Parks and Wildlife Service's wide-ranging website, includes national parks, nature reserves, protected sites, and hundreds of publications.

pinemarten.ie information on pine martens in Ireland, for householders, journalists, gun clubs, foresters and farmers (Vincent Wildlife Trust Ireland and National Parks and Wildlife Service).

pollinators.ie the All-Ireland Pollinator Plan: advice on managing the landscape for pollinators, creating and maintaining habitats, information on bees, hoverflies and other pollinators.

raisedbogs.ie The Living Bog, Irish bog restoration project, detailing history, wildlife and other information for each site.

rspb.org.uk the Royal Society for the Protection of Birds: comprehensive information on birds in Britain and Northern Ireland (birds do not observe boundaries, so most of the knowledge applies to all of Ireland).

sealrescueireland.org information on seal rescue operations, volunteering, seal species.

sharktrust.org British Shark Trust: information on shark, ray and skate species.

swiftconservation.ie advice and information about conservation actions for swifts in Ireland.

thehsi.org the Herpetological Society of Ireland: information on our native amphibians and our lone reptile, the common lizard.

vincentwildlife.ie organisation supporting wildlife conservation in Ireland; species profiles of Irish land mammals.

wildaboutgardens.org.uk advice on wildlife gardening and how to support nature at home (Royal Horticultural Society and Wildlife Trusts).

wildflowersofireland.net Zoë Devlin's wildflower site: find plants by colour, name, family or month of flower, illustrated with thousands of photos.

woodlandtrust.org.uk information on woodland trees, habitats and wildlife.

xeno-canto.org collaborative project featuring hundreds of thousands of recordings of bird sounds from all over the world.

Social media

Many of the organisations above have Facebook, Twitter and Instagram profiles where you can interact with them and like-minded people.

Hashtags

#MothsMatter moth-related tweets, mostly from Britain and Ireland.

#TwitterNatureCommunity nature-related tweets from Britain and Ireland.

#wildflowerhour takes place (mainly on Twitter) 8–9 p.m. Sunday, featuring wildflowers found in Britain and Ireland.

Apps

Biodiversity Data Capture (Compass Informatics Ltd): National Biodiversity Data Centre's app for recording while you are out and about. Sightings are added to the centre's repository of records.

British & Irish Bumblebees (NatureGuides Ltd): field guide to 23 bumblebee species in Britain and Ireland (paid).

British Trees (Woodland Trust): free interactive app for identifying 78 common trees, both native and introduced.

Collins Bird Guide (NatureGuides Ltd) and iBird UK Pro Guide to Birds (Mitch Waite Group): two bird ID apps for UK and Ireland, both include diagnostic drawings, photos, calls and songs, range maps. Collins includes a facility for making lists (both are paid apps).

eBird (Cornell Lab of Ornithology): free app for recording bird sightings worldwide; shows hotspots and lists of birds.

Eggcase Hunt (Shark Trust): free app for identifying and recording egg cases of the shark family.

iBird UK and Ireland Lite (Mitch Waite Group): free birding app, contains 40 common birds.

Moths of Britain and Ireland and The Moths of Britain and Ireland (NatureGuides Ltd): two moth ID apps; the first, with photos, is based on Manley's book; the second, with illustrations, based on Waring and Townsend's field guide (both are paid apps).

Bibliography

Anderson, Glynn, *Birds of Ireland, Facts, Folklore & History*, The Collins Press, 2008

Balmer, Dawn (co-ordinator), *Bird Atlas 2007–11: The Breeding and Wintering Birds of Britain and Ireland*, HarperCollins Publishers, 2013

Bradbury, Kate, *Wildlife Gardening*, Bloomsbury Publishing, 2019

Cabot, David, *Ireland: A Natural History*, first edn: William Collins, 1999, this edn: William Collins Kindle, 2018

Chinery, Michael, *Collins Nature Guide: Garden Wildlife of Britain and Europe*, HarperCollins, 2001

Culpeper, Nicholas, *Culpeper's Complete Herbal*, first edn: 1653, this edn: Wordsworth, 1995

Dempsey, Eric and O'Clery, Michael, *Finding Birds in Ireland: The Complete Guide*, Gill & Macmillan, 2007

Devlin, Zoë, *Wildflowers of Ireland*, The Collins Press, 2011

Doogue, Declan and Krieger, Carsten, *The Wild Flowers of Ireland: The Habitat Guide*, Gill & Macmillan, 2010

Edwards, Mike and Jenner, Martin, *Field Guide to the Bumblebees of Great Britain & Ireland*, Ocelli, 2005

Fennell, Aubrey, *Heritage Trees of Ireland*, The Collins Press, 2013

Fitzpatrick, Úna, Weekes, Lynda and Wright, Mark, *Ireland's Biodiversity Identification Guide to Ireland's Grasses*, National Biodiversity Data Centre, 2016

Fraser, Patrick Neill, *List of British Ferns and their varieties*, Neill & Co., 1868

Gerard, John, *The Herball or Generall Historie of Plantes*, John Norton, 1597

Greer, Heather, *On Your Doorstep: Moths and Butterflies of Connemara*, Matador, 2016

Grieve, Mrs M., *A Modern Herbal*, first edn: Jonathan Cape Ltd., 1931, this edn: Tiger Books International, 1992

Grigson, Geoffrey, *The Englishman's Flora*, first edn: Phoenix House, 1958, this edn: Helicon, 1996

Hart, Henry Chichester, *Flora of the County Donegal*, Sealy, Bryers and Walker, 1898

Hatfield, Gabrielle, *Hatfield's Herbal: The Secret History of British Plants*, Allen Lane, Penguin, 2007

Hayman, Peter and Hume, Rob, *Bird: The Ultimate Illustrated Guide to the Birds of Britain and Europe*, Mitchell Beazley, 2007

Jebb, Matthew and Crowley, Colm (eds), *Secrets of the Irish Landscape*, Atrium, 2013

K'Eogh, John, *Zoologia Medicinalis Hibernica: Or, A Treatise of Birds, Beasts, Fishes, Reptiles, Or Insects*, S. Powell, 1739

Kirke Swann, H., *A Dictionary of English and Folk-Names of British Birds*, Witherby & Co, 1913

Læssøe, Thomas, *Mushrooms*, Dorling Kindersley, 1998

Lysaght, Liam and Marnell, Ferdia (eds), *Atlas of Mammals in Ireland: 2010–2015*, National Biodiversity Data Centre, 2016

Mabey, Richard, *Flora Britannica*, Sinclair-Stevenson, 1996

McAlister, Erica, *The Secret Life of Flies*, Natural History Museum, 2017

Mackay, James Townsend, *Flora Hibernica*, William Curry June and Co., 1836

Mac Coitir, Niall, *Ireland's Animals*, The Collins Press, 2010

Mac Coitir, Niall, *Irish Trees: Myths, Legends & Folklore*, The Collins Press, 2003

Mac Coitir, Niall, *Irish Wild Plants: Myths, Legends & Folklore*, The Collins Press, 2006

McCormack, Stephen and Regan, Eugenie: *Insects of Ireland*, The Collins Press, 2014

McGeehan, Anthony and Wyllie, Julian, *Birds of the Homeplace*, The Collins Press, 2014

McGeehan, Anthony, *To the Ends of the Earth: Ireland's Place in Bird Migration*, The Collins Press, 2018

Marren, Peter and Mabey, Richard, *Bugs Britannica*, Chatto & Windus, 2010

Moore, David and More, Alexander Goodman, *Contributions towards a Cybele Hibernica*, 1866

Moss, Stephen, *Do Birds Have Knees? All Your Bird Questions Answered*, Bloomsbury Publishing, 2016

Mulvihill, Mary, *Ingenious Ireland*, 2nd edn, Four Courts Press, 2019

Nelson, E. Charles and Walsh, Wendy F., *The Burren: A Companion to the Wildflowers of an Irish Limestone Wilderness*, The Conservancy of the Burren, 1997

Nelson, E. Charles and Walsh, Wendy F., *Trees of Ireland: Native and Naturalized*, Lilliput Press, 1993

Ní Lamhna, Éanna, *Wild Dublin: Exploring Nature in the City*, O'Brien, 2008

O'Sullivan, Oran and Wilson, Jim, *Ireland's Garden Birds: How to Identify, Attract & Garden for Birds*, The Collins Press, 2008

Parnell, John and Curtis, Tom, *Webb's: An Irish Flora*, 8th edn, Cork University Press, 2012

Pilcher, Jonathan and Hall, Valerie, *Flora Hibernica: The Wild Flowers, Plants and Trees of Ireland*, The Collins Press, 2001

Praeger, Robert Lloyd, *The Way That I Went*, first edn: Hodges, Figgis and Co., 1937, this edn: Allen Figgis Ltd., 1969

Reynolds, Sylvia C. P., *A Catalogue of Alien Plants in Ireland*, National Botanic Gardens, Glasnevin, 2002

Robinson, William, *The English Flower Garden*, 5th edn, John Murray, 1897

Rutty, John, *An Essay towards the Natural History of the County of Dublin*, vol. 1, W. Sleater, 1772

Scannell, M. J. P. and Synnott, D. M., *Census Catalogue of the Flora of Ireland*, The Stationery Office, Dublin, 1972

Scharff, R. F., 'The Slugs of Ireland', The Scientific Transactions of the Royal Dublin Society, vol. 4, series 2, 1891

Sex, Susan and Sayers, Brendan, *Ireland's Wild Orchids: A Field Guide*, privately published, printed by Nicholson and Bass, 2009

Sex, Susan and Sayers, Brendan, *Ireland's Wild Orchids*, privately published, 2004

Stearn, William T., *Stearn's Dictionary of Plant Names for Gardeners*, 2nd edn, Cassell, 1992

Swainson, Rev. Charles, *Provincial Names and Folk Lore of British Birds*, Trübner and Co., 1885

Taylor, Lucy and Nickelsen, Emma, *Ireland's Seashore: A Field Guide*, The Collins Press, 2018

Threlkeld, Caleb, *Synopsis Stirpium Hibernicarum*, first edn: S. Powell, 1726, this edn: Boethius Press, 1988

Ussher, Richard J. and Warren, Robert, *The Birds of Ireland*, Gurney and Jackson, 1900

Vickery, Roy, *A Dictionary of Plant-Lore*, Oxford University Press, 1995

Walsh, Wendy and Nelson, Charles, *An Irish Florilegium II: Wild and Garden Plants of Ireland*, Thames and Hudson, 1987

Watters, John J., *The Natural History of the Birds of Ireland*, James McGlashan, 1853

Whelan, Paul, *Lichens of Ireland*, The Collins Press, 2011

Whittingham, Sarah, *Fern Fever: The Story of Pteridomania*, Frances Lincoln Ltd., 2012

Wilson, Jim and Carmody, Mark, *The Birds of Ireland: A Field Guide*, The Collins Press, 2013

Wyse Jackson, Peter, *Ireland's Generous Nature: The Past and Present Uses of Wild Plants in Ireland*, Missouri Botanical Garden Press, St. Louis, 2014

Index